Growing the Elephant offers road
cal support to you in maximizin̤͛
working well together across the lines of real and perceived
differences in our workplaces. Read and share to deepen
your understanding of privilege and how to use it – and possibly transform it – for good.

Rhonda Magee, M.A., J.D., author of *The Inner*
Work of Racial Justice

Chris and Gloria brilliantly weave together insights and tools
from mindfulness, competitiveness, and change to the challenge of DEI. By delineating the assumptions and actions
of earned vs. unearned advantage and by learning from the
four archetypes, this book dramatically advances how people
in any setting grow and relate to each other. Amazing book:
clever, insightful, relevant, and actionable.

Dave Ulrich, Rensis Likert Professor, Ross School of
Business, University of Michigan
Partner, The RBL Group

This groundbreaking book offers a new and exciting par-
adigm for enhancing diversity training. Using a model of
earned versus unearned advantage, which seems eminently
sensible and wise to me, it weaves in contemplative and mindfulness practices so that we are not stuck in "now what do I
do?" with no place for healing or action. This book is the
"now what." I am confident the wisdom and compassion of
this methodology will be used widely for the benefit of many.

Diana Winston, Director of Mindfulness Education at
UCLA's Mindful Awareness Research Center and
author of *The Little Book of Being*

Years ago, I was with Chris Altizer in that DEI workshop in
the story. Like Chris, I didn't like how I felt then, either.

Life experiences and the practices in this book have helped me begin to get square with my own unearned advantages. I believe this book opens the mind and the heart and can help all of us, whoever you are or wherever you're from, face the elephant in the room and grow earned advantage – for everyone.

Jeff Kindler, CEO, Centrexion Therapeutics

As a Latina who has led many nonprofits committed to creating opportunities for all, I continue to apply really important life lessons about privilege or what this book quite appropriately calls "unearned advantage." Many more of us need deeper understanding because, then, we can do better problem-solving. As I read this book, I recall moments when Gloria, a co-author, and I, would exchange smiles of appreciation when someone other than us – who was not of color or not a woman – would call out the "elephant" in that room of national CEOs where we gathered for several years. I don't think it's a coincidence that our most productive discussions happened when individuals of different identities had taken the time to learn. Whether you are a CEO, board member, staff member, or community volunteer, your time will be well spent reading and reflecting on the rich insights you'll find here.

Anna Maria Chavez, Chief Impact Officer; President, Encantos Foundation; Board Chair; Founder, Fearless Global Girl Initiative; Former National CEO, Girl Scouts of America

At a time of increasing public debate around the topic of equality and after many organizations' well intended, but often ineffective attempts to move the needle with DE&I training, Chris and Gloria offer a meaningful shift in the discourse and reframing of the discussion. Rather than zero-sum thinking, they demonstrate a practical and actionable approach utilizing a growth mindset. Their book is a thought-provoking prescription for advancing DE&I by growing earned advantage for all.

Michael Goettler, CEO, Viatris Inc.

Our unwillingness to discuss the topic advantage has created a culture where it's simply avoided – like a huge elephant in the room. Chris and Gloria invite readers to examine "the elephant" through a compassionate mix of stories and practices that open the mind and the heart. In a time of increased division and decreasing dialogue, when discussions of inequality are so difficult they are becoming legislated, Chris and Gloria bring a different approach to how we address it – from the inside – out. This book meets people wherever they are without judgment as they explore the elephant and helps us all find ways to grow earned advantage for everyone.

Shelly Tygielski, author of *Sit Down to Rise Up: How Radical Self-Care Can Change the World* and Founder, Pandemic of Love

After the senseless murder of George Floyd, I had the opportunity to speak with many African-Americans who shared gut wrenching and heartbreaking stories. Stories describing what it was like raising their children, needing to give them the "talk" about how to behave if they were pulled over and how they worried for their children. I also heard from White Americans that wanted to reach out to their Black friends—especially those in the workplace, knowing that they were hurting, but afraid to broach the subject.

This practical and impactful book gives people the tools they need to address these issues. It describes the journey that we can take together to better understand each other in a way that is helpful, effective and meaningful. The tone is not accusatory; rather it strives for being understanding of each other. We can all learn from reading *Growing the Elephant.*

Gail J. McGovern, President and CEO,
American Red Cross

As a DEI consultant with 30 years of experience evaluating existing and creating new DEI programming, this book provides a major alternative to the focus on the damages resulting in inequality by instead focusing on preventing the impact of inequality through positive approaches and solutions to support everyone, regardless of advantage. It also provides a methodology to prevent negative impacts and promote equal advantage for all.

Kent D. Lollis, Esq., DEI and Educational Consultant;
LSAC DEI Vice President Emeritus

Theory tells us that a more diverse workforce can lead to better decision making, greater organizational vitality, and long-term success. But what are the practical steps organizations must take to realize these benefits? For everyone who has lived through the shortcomings of traditional DEI programs and seminars and avoided them ever since, Chris Altizer and Gloria Johnson-Cusack provide a new approach. Based on extensive interviews and research, their approach uses contemplation, meditation, and mindfulness techniques to stimulate personal growth and discovery. Not a silver bullet, but an approach that, with time and concerted effort, can produce insights among individual employees and breakthroughs for their organizations.

Larry Stimpert, Ph.D., President,
Hampden-Sydney College; Author

Growing the Elephant

Increasing earned advantage for all

CHRIS ALTIZER & GLORIA JOHNSON-CUSACK

First published in Great Britain by Practical Inspiration Publishing, 2022

ISBN   9781788603881   (print)
       9781788603904   (epub)
       9781788603898   (mobi)

Illustrations by Maria Laura Garza, Nahaus Inc.

Want to bulk-buy copies of this book for your team and colleagues? We can introduce case studies, customize the content and co-brand *Growing the Elephant* to suit your business's needs.

Please email info@practicalinspiration.com for more details.

Practical Inspiration
Publishing

Contents

Foreword

This book is profoundly simple. It breaks down the complexity of some of the most difficult DEI issues with clear and compelling exercises and well-documented research. Reading and experiencing this book provides us with less of a "how to" but more of a "how to be" path. The shared, lived experiences of this team of amalgamated characters, many of whom I felt I've known and been, represent ourselves and others we know. Their stories allow the reader to navigate a journey to understanding how to "increase earned advantage for everyone."

The new language and frameworks in *Growing the Elephant* help demystify current jargon and provide real and accessible ways to enhance our understanding of ourselves and each other. The approach avoids the over-intellectualization that can come with this work, leaving people uncertain about what to actually *do* – whatever their level of advantage. After all, it all begins with self-recognition and acceptance of our own individual unearned advantages. From there we are unstoppable, individually and collectively.

This is all about increasing earned advantage for everyone and is a model I will use for boards and staff. I commend the authors, especially Gloria, with whom I had the unique and meaningful opportunity to work with as President of the Council on Foundations. This book is a "must" resource and most relevant – right now.

Vikki Spruill, President and CEO, New England Aquarium,
Former President and CEO, Council on Foundations

Prologue

"Thank God THAT'S over," thought Robert. The mandated session on diversity, equity, and inclusion, or DEI, had crumbled to a close, and participants made their way out of the room without any discussion. Robert had hoped the session wouldn't be the complete waste of time his work friends had warned him about, but it seemed destined to go sideways from the start. "This 'privilege' thing," he later told a friend, "is crap! I earned what I have, and no one can tell me different!"

Maria also left the session unhappy – not so much angry as conflicted. "I'm feeling confused about what should be a simple thing," she thought. Maria had always known that she was treated differently than the friends she knew as a child in Venezuela because her skin and hair were lighter than theirs and because she came from a family of means. "I guess that helps me – but am I supposed to feel bad? I can't help how I was born! Now, if I were born a brother instead of a sister, I'd be doing even better!"

"If one more person asks me to explain what it's like to be Black in America, I'm just going to collapse!" Yvonne was exhausted – again. Her entire working life, Yvonne had always been one of the few minority females in the room and felt a spotlight on her each time discussions about equality came up. "Most of the time, they (those asking) mean well, but it's like they're asking a question in English but hearing my answer in a foreign language – they just can't understand what I'm saying!"

And Alvin? Alvin was familiar with the concepts and terms used in the program – and with some of the reactions of others. "We studied issues of race, history, and social justice in school," he said. "But at school, it was easier to talk about it. It seemed like each of us could 'be' who we are without posing to be someone else. The working world doesn't feel like that. And since this COVID thing, I think some people seem to be avoiding me."

After the seminar, the facilitator sighed. "It's like driving a bus with ten different GPS systems, each giving me different routes while randomly screaming, 'recalibrating route!'" This facilitator could relate to all four of these participants – upset, confused, exhausted, and afraid to share that she didn't have the correct GPS route herself.

> *"It's like driving a bus with ten different GPS systems, each giving me different routes while randomly screaming, 'recalibrating route!'"*

A word from the authors

Chris

After a few decades in human resources, consulting, and university teaching, I've met and, at times, felt like each of these folks – embarrassed to be privileged, exhausted by the divides, confused about what I believe, and covering all those beliefs when in certain company. While I relate mostly to Robert, through research, interviews, and collaboration we've tried to reflect the many more personae beyond those we've developed for this story. Each of us faces the difficult subject of who has and doesn't have advantages in life. Some of us turn away from it, and some sneak a peek. Some charge at it, and some say what others want to hear. And some freeze, hoping it will all go away. Unfortunately, not enough of us are standing and facing it for what it is – which is why it hasn't gotten better.

Robert's experience in the seminar may be familiar to those like him – or like me. The description of Robert's experience was my own experience in 2005 when I worked at Pfizer, Inc. as a VP of Human Resources. Up to that point, I perceived my role in diversity and inclusion similar to Dr. Stefanie K. Johnson's description of the *White Knight* archetype in her outstanding book *Inclusify*.[1] I was a "defender and champion"

---

[1] Stefanie K. Johnson, *Inclusify: The Power of Uniqueness and Belonging to Build Innovative Teams.* Harper Business, 2020.

of women; Black, indigenous, and people of color (BIPOC); Lesbian, Gay, Bisexual, Transgender, and Queer (LGBTQ); and anyone else not like me. I felt pretty good about being called an "ally" and "advocate." Noble? I thought so. Effective? Mostly in making me feel good about myself while ignoring the unearned advantages I had accrued and leveraged in my life. I was, it turns out, seeking acknowledgement of my good intentions, or "cookies," as brilliantly described by Dolly Chugh in *The Person You Mean to Be.*[2] But at that point, I did not recognize it.

It's been a decade-plus path to seeing it as clearly as I do now – which is still foggy but improving. That evolving clarity, the frightening events of the last few years, and dissatisfaction with how we're all dealing with it all sparked the notion of the elephant. It also provided the opportunity to collaborate with and learn from my brilliant co-author Gloria Johnson-Cusack to bring forward this book.

Denying, ignoring, or papering over these challenges has not only not worked but has brought us collectively to boiling point in cities and workplaces globally. The approaches of the last few decades ranging from "everyone's equal" to calling out "privilege" have not advanced equality or improved inclusion. Our fictional team's experience described earlier is too real and too familiar – anger, confusion, exhaustion, covering. Without the ability to safely engage in the difficult conversation, our team – and we – find ourselves stuck in the situation of having to discuss tough issues without a path forward. Without a path forward, we get the reactions we read about, observe, and even experience, including outright denial, deliberate division, active discrimination, and the rare but frightening outbursts of violence.

---

[2] Dolly Chugh, *The Person You Mean to Be: How Good People Fight Bias.* HarperCollins, 2018.

The history, old and recent, around the world and in the United States highlights how hard this continues to be. In our example, Alvin's truth was as valid as Yvonne's, Maria's, and Robert's. Is it possible to shift from "calling out" to "calling in"? Can we create opportunities to "open up" rather than "shut down"? The route that's been followed for decades hasn't led to a better place. There's an elephant in the room that we continue to ignore. As Einstein is famously, if not correctly quoted as saying, insanity is doing the same thing repeatedly and expecting different results. How can we get sane?

Gloria

I relate to every single character in this book. That's because I have needed to make choices through most of my life to try to be a changemaker and servant leader who builds bridges. It's that choicemaking or else I live angry and sad about the historical and persistent reality of unconscious bias.

As a person of color, who came from a racially segregated background in the United States and moved from being middle class to working poor and then decidedly privileged during my adult life, I experienced and witnessed unconscious bias and its ugly consequences. Most of my childhood was marked by little to no healthcare nor financial cushion from family disasters. This was true even though both of my parents held master's degrees and all three of my siblings worked jobs constantly, like me, since age 14. In contrast, most of my adult life is marked by holding highly privileged positions in business, nonprofits, faith-based organizations, higher education, government, and philanthropy. While all those organizations are meant to be service oriented, we often fell short because individuals in leadership – the people who usually are the drivers of sustainable change – lacked sufficient awareness of unconscious bias. As a result, we missed rich opportunities to do something about it by growing what we call in this book "earned advantage" to expand opportunities for everyone.

Unconscious bias is like a cluster of sleeper cancer cells found in all human beings. If fed, these cancer cells multiply and eat at our hearts to make us myopic and self-concerned. They spread to eat at our minds to make us unimaginative when problem-solving. I was well into my career as an executive when I understood deeply that I can manage my own unconscious biases and provide strategic counsel to help other leaders and their boards and teams be more intentional. The fact is that I personally suffered the consequences of historical disparate treatment of people of color in the United States. An equally important fact is that I experienced support from great human beings of many races in this country – a country I continue to believe is great. Some of my strongest allies have been people with completely different beliefs, backgrounds, and identities – people who often are totally nervous all the way through! These allies in all sectors of our communities feed my soul and help me grow as a changemaker who is emotionally healthy and inspired.

Just as I continue to do, each of the characters in this book in some way must recognize the painful realities of unconscious bias. When we do that, we sometimes are angry because this recognition means we no longer can think of ourselves as we want to. We are sad because this recognition makes it difficult to be optimistic – whether about ourselves or others, in both our personal and our public lives. In the public sphere, changes in policies and systems are always essential to achieve diversity, equity and inclusion that is sustainable and reaches many people at-scale. Equally essential are positive changes in the hearts and minds of individuals

– individuals who agitate for systemic change and individuals who use their power in the public sphere to increase earned advantage. Some of my struggles and failures are captured in our characters' stories but so too are many stories about individuals' growth and impact through humility and courage.

Chris, my co-author and fellow journeyman, joins me in believing deeply that we can, in fact, pursue well-founded optimism as long as we as individuals set our intentions to be the change we want to see. Talent is equally distributed throughout the world, but opportunity is not. For us, there is deep joy in providing support and guidance to many people of goodwill.

A word to leaders

For leaders or supporting experts who are already convinced that more DEI is a good thing and want to jump in as quickly as possible or throw others in and ask them if it worked, take a breath. This book begins with you. The intended awareness, reflections, insights, and even discomforts can't be delegated or assigned. *Growing the Elephant* isn't a playbook of DEI tactics or store of quick fixes, nor is there a Cliff notes version that bypasses the work. Our advice, based on decades of experience and hard lessons, is to read and work with the book before you require others to read it. When you have begun to recognize and work with sources of advantage, you'll find growing earned advantage, and engaging others in the discussion, comes more easily.

For leaders and supporting experts who are exhausted by, annoyed with, or skeptical about DEI work, also take a breath. This book also begins with you. The practices you'll try and the Growth Advantage Mindset you'll read about aren't trying to brainwash you or change your values. *Growing the Elephant* isn't a morality play or guilt trip – it's about increasing earned advantage for everyone. Our advice, also based on personal experiences, is to not skip over the reflection exercises or read them like a word problem to solve. Whatever you think, feel, recall, or imagine, it's OK. Whatever mindset you find in yourself along the way, it's OK. If you read and practice all this and don't see a need to change, it's OK. The fact that you're reading this right now gives us hope that you'll keep walking the path.

Introduction: Introducing the elephant

The analogy of the elephant is about that thing people didn't want to talk about, "the elephant in the room," unearned advantage. As our DEI workshop participants and facilitator each found, the typical approaches to talking about DEI topics, particularly privilege, have not proven particularly effective. In researching and writing this book, we believe we need to rethink our approach. We need a way to bring people together in awareness and conversation. We need a safe, brave way to raise our individual awareness and understanding of advantages so we can collectively expand, or grow, the opportunity to increase them. In *competition*, we seek to corner advantage to be in a superior position over a challenge or an opponent. But in a *community*, we are hopefully in cooperation and share a desire to *grow* advantage, so we all are in a superior position over our challenges and not each other.

The intention and outcome of building and strengthening "community" in this sense is developing more and better solutions. Literally, every endeavor of a team has the potential to yield better outcomes than we ever imagine when we expand individual awareness and understanding of advantage. This expansion is the goal of various initiatives and programs, often under the banner of "diversity, equity, and inclusion," or "DEI." *Growing the Elephant* wasn't created to replace DEI programs or approaches but to increase an individual's ability to learn while growing earned advantage. By growing the elephant of earned advantage in a community – any community of any size – that community optimizes performance potential and increases efficiencies of communication and collaboration.

This isn't a new revelation to organizations and teams – whether they are based in the United States, like our fictional team, or elsewhere. The advantages of leveraging diversity through inclusion have been widely recognized, if not often successfully reaped, for decades. To gain the benefits of diversity, we need to understand sources of advantage. Sources of advantage aren't new, but how we think of and talk about them needs to change. We need to recognize the elephant in the room – the elephant of advantage.

In *Growing the Elephant*, we recognize that this elephant of advantage has two kinds of advantages. We will explore and define advantage in tangible terms of *Earned* and *Unearned* advantage. Robert's reaction to his seminar experience is typical of most human beings, "If I have something good, it's because I earned it." Maybe through good work, or demonstrated talent or hard work, or the grace of a higher being – I earned it. Starting a seminar or discussion with, "No, you didn't!" doesn't work with anyone – regardless of who they are or where they are from. The challenge is that most past and current programs or experiences don't allow and explore differences between earned and unearned advantages. Exploring this difference is key to opening the door to safe-yet-brave discussions, awareness, and positive action.

Growing the Elephant – our approach and intent

The research behind this book includes scores of interviews, the work of cited experts, and the lived experiences of the authors. It's written out of some dissatisfaction and a sense of opportunity with past and current offerings in diversity, equity, and inclusion. *Growing the Elephant* is written to be felt and experienced – not always comfortable but always manageable.

Our approach in *Growing the Elephant* acknowledges some common terms and concepts you can find in most DEI programs like "privilege" and "unconscious biases." And we also introduce practices that may be new to you. Another gap in past and current programs, and one we intend to address in this book, is providing some different but simple ways that help you effectively reflect on what you're exploring and stay with it – even when it's uncomfortable. These have begun to emerge in recent years through works and experts we'll cite as we go along.

In writing and researching this book, we recognized and took in the diversity of views on the history, causes, and drivers of unearned advantage, particularly in the United States. The concept of "intersectionality," or the layered up or stacked deficit of unearned advantages, is reflected in the story. While the reality of systemic political, economic, and societal factors is not lost on us, we focus on how each individual can grow the elephant of earned advantage. *Growing the Elephant* centers on each individual's reflection, growth, and action to increase earned advantage and strives to meet each reader where they are in their daily life.

We'll be introducing these practices throughout the book and strongly encourage you to work with them along the way. Whether you're wildly into, completely uninterested, or skeptical about practices of reflection, mindfulness, or meditation, these exercises will be valuable in developing your insights and ability to be with what you see. If you remain skeptical, we appreciate the open-mindedness that carries you to and through the book! We hope that you might feel more informed about emerging practices that many people find valuable, if not essential, in an increasingly polarized world.

> *Whether you're wildly into, completely uninterested, or skeptical about practices of reflection, mindfulness, or meditation, these exercises will be valuable in developing your insights and ability to be with what you see.*

We are indebted to the works and training of Rhonda Magee, Jon Kabat-Zinn, Rick Hanson, and others with whom we have studied or from whom we have learned and invite you to expand your ability to deal with uncomfortable things through their work. You can find more about their work in the Additional Reading section at the end of the book.

The primary outcomes we intend from this book are for you to *recognize, work with,* and *grow opportunities* for earned advantage. From that, we hope you will apply what you learn in the communities or teams in which you live and work. This journey through advantage will take many steps.

This image illustrates the idea that both kinds of advantage exist and have an impact. It also illustrates that practicing recognizing and working with unearned advantage creates space to grow earned advantage.

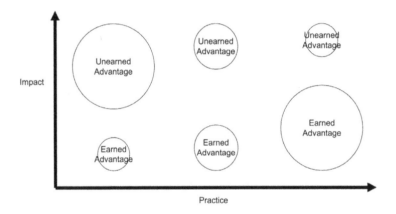

Our intention is to grow the opportunities for earned advantage for you and those around you. As you'll discover, this requires understanding and addressing the opportunities influenced by unearned advantage. Teaser – you'll notice unearned advantage does not shrink to oblivion. It can't – and we'll explain why.

An approach to reading this book

Our goal is to stimulate thought, reflection, and action of our audiences. You may be reading this book from a passion, curiosity, or even skepticism about your understanding of diversity, equity, and inclusion. You may be the leader in an organization, a facilitator or practitioner of learning, or someone who's been invited or even assigned to read this to stimulate what you expect to be uncomfortable conversations. You may be a demographic minority or majority in any category of difference. Who you are and where you're from does, as you'll find, matter. This book is for all these and more. It's for you.

As we said, we'll introduce a variety of practices as you recognize, work with, and grow earned advantage. It's challenging to reflect on a difficult question and many find it difficult to sit in reflection on any question! If a few minutes of reflection doesn't come easily, try it in smaller bits at a time. If you find yourself getting frustrated or wanting to bounce, give yourself a break. Then come back. This book can take weeks or even longer to work through. It's not a sprint (see *How to Eat an Elephant*, p. 161 in the Resources section). You may find there are things you want to talk about with others – we encourage that! You may find you want to talk with and listen to people just like or different from you at different points – we encourage that as well.

Another challenge – especially for people who define themselves as patriotic, family oriented, and community minded – is our difficulty reconciling knowledge about past wrongs with our desire to believe our shared world, country, organization, team, and neighbors are better than facts would suggest. Often, when confronted with difficult facts about past or present practices, we hear voices in our heads saying, "Wait a minute, I love my country, my family, my community. It just seems wrong and even disloyal to have too many conversations about things that make us lose our pride in who WE are!" Take heart. There's a good chance you will feel even more pride in yourself, your community, and your country as you see how possible it is for every person to grow in understanding. Sometimes, maybe now, it's YOU asking the small-but-big question that unlocks the "aha" for every-one in your group. Sometimes, asking yourself or someone else is all there is to "do."

This raises yet another challenge for many reading this book – feeling the need "to DO" something! Leaders, in particular, want to know the answer and get to solving the problem. *Growing the Elephant* is about building necessary skills and insights to get to the "What now? What next?" to increase earned advantage. There will be moments of wonder, frustration, and insight. Stick with it. This is a walk with a destination – but it takes each step to get there.

Another (*really, another one!?*) challenge in reading this book is anticipating the different ways that different people approach these difficult subjects. Some lead with the intellectual, others with the emotional. You will find it touches both. Some will read for content and skip the exercises. The value is much more in the experience than the knowledge. Some will scan for what validates their experience or waves a red flag that they will not abide. You will likely find both.

With these challenges, as if you didn't have enough to do already, why read this book?

- Even if you believe right now that the distinctions between earned and unearned advantage are over-blown, overused, or over-hyped, you'll know how people leaning in with greater intentionality are en-couraging others to do it.
- Even if you don't yet know what to DO from wher-ever you sit, you'll know how to recognize sources of earned and unearned advantage.
- Even if you are encouraged/required to read this book and don't value or do the exercises, you'll get the point that the work is emotional, tough, and essential.

- Even if team members you are working with choose NOT to do the exercises, you will likely benefit from the exercises – likely more so!

Some readers approach these subjects from a performance imperative, others from a moral imperative. Some balance these things evenly, others have a priority. To be clear, our collective experience is that growing earned advantage increases competitive advantage through increased innovation and collaboration. This is true for individuals, organizations, and communities.

> *To be clear, our collective experience is that growing earned advantage increases competitive advantage through increased innovation and collaboration. This is true for individuals, organizations, and communities.*

However you approach these difficult subjects, you can apply your approach while you experiment with what's uncomfortable.

And it's not always comfortable.

Growing – not always comfortable

Similar to how growth spurts in childhood are sometimes awkward and even uncomfortable, learnings, even as adults, that challenge beliefs or experiences can have the same effect. Whether you're reading this book on your own or with others, there may be points where you feel stretched. That's intentional. If you don't find yourself at some points challenged, wondering, skeptical, or even bothered, you're not learning anything new, just reinforcing what you already believe. Regardless of who you are or where you're from, the exercises in this book may stimulate you out of your comfort zone. The point where you go beyond what you already know or believe – your comfort zone – is the learning or "growth" zone. In the growth zone, you are *rationally* processing new information or perspectives. This is, of course, work! And not just the intellectual kind.

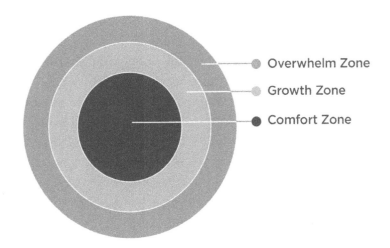

Overwhelm Zone

Growth Zone

Comfort Zone

Image credit: Maria Laura Garza

The "rational" part isn't a given. Just as physical growth spurts are uncomfortable, new information or perspectives that challenge your mind are, too. The mind can trip from the growth zone into the panic or "overwhelm" zone. The overwhelm zone is the point past where the mind loses the ability to think about or evaluate what's happening and flips into a stress-induced response. This isn't an intellectual response but an emotional one where emotions of anger, resentment, envy, fear, or guilt create sensations of being gored, trampled, whipped, or trumpeted. How can we avoid that?

First, recognize that the purpose of *Growing the Elephant* is not to change your mind about what you believe but to inform your perspective, conclusions, and actions from your own experience. This book isn't trying to tell you what to think; you are your best teacher. If nothing else, the practices in this book may help you face and manage difficult situations – of any kind.

Second, recognize that you are able to choose where you are within each zone, and even change the sizes of them. You have the ability to choose to be in your comfort or your growth zone when it suits you. Sometimes we just need to chill out in the comfort zone mentally and emotionally – that's human. That said, the more often you choose your growth zone, the bigger your comfort zone becomes. The more often you choose your growth zone, the more space you have before hitting your overwhelm zone. And while you don't choose your overwhelm zone, the practices in this book will help you come back from it. Our ability to respond to what we experience rather than automatically react to it is also human, but we need to develop that ability for it to be available when we need it most.

We will talk more about these reactions throughout the book. We point this out in the beginning because we also present to you various practices that can help you move between the comfort and growth zones as you go. The practices increase your ability in the moment to face the discomfort of the growth zone.

Rather than read about and evaluate these practices to (maybe) try later, we strongly encourage you *to practice them as you go.* As you explore this elephant, you will almost certainly have thoughts or reactions that might kick you from growth into overwhelm. Along with increasing your ability to face the inevitable discomforts of the growth zone, these practices can help you stop short of the overwhelm zone or step back from it if you trip into it. If you read this book in one sitting, you're an engaged reader, but you probably missed the experience.

This journey isn't easy – it can't be. The challenges we're facing aren't, so the solutions aren't, either. If at any point you feel overwhelmed or challenged beyond your ability to move on, take a break and resource yourself as you know how. If the stories, exercises, reflections, or conversations with others bring up painful or aggravating thoughts or feelings, consider talking with a trusted advisor or counselor who can support you. You wouldn't go on a long hike without water and good shoes – and this will be a hike.

We will introduce some practices to help you be with uncomfortable thoughts and emotions throughout the book. You may know these already or find them novel. You may find you learn something from trying them, whether you feel you need them or not. Before you go on, consider taking a breath.

Expansive breathing — it's a big breath...

Also known as the three-part breath, this breath utilizes all breathing spaces in the body, emptying and filling the lungs to their fullest capacity. Full, deep breathing stimulates the parasympathetic nervous system, slowing the heart rate and lowering blood pressure. So begin the practice without big pauses and stay in your comfort zone!

Inhaling:

1. Inhale through the nose and allow the breath to expand the belly out to its fullest. This fills the abdominal or lower portion of the lungs.

2. Feel the inhalation of air rising, and allow the rib cage to expand. This is the middle of the lungs.
3. Continue to the end of the inhalation, directing the breath into the upper chest and the collarbone area. This is the upper part of the lungs.
4. Allow a natural pause with the lungs completely full.

Exhaling:

1. At a pace slower than your inhale, exhale from the upper chest, feeling the collarbone relax or lower.
2. Exhale further to allow the midchest to relax and lower.
3. Draw the abdomen in, engaging the abdominal muscles to complete the entire exhalation.

Repeat once or twice. How do you feel?

We suggest practicing this breath a few times a day and paying attention to the sensations of expansion and contraction of the entire thoracic region.

Some terms and the team

We'll be using some terms throughout the book that you may have heard or used. We'll also be defining a few in a particular way that may be different for you – some of them follow here:

Advantage – "a superiority of position or condition; a factor or circumstance of benefit to its possessor."[1]

- **Earned advantage** – benefits or position gained or granted based on what you do without regard to who you are.
- **Unearned advantage** – benefits or position gained or granted by virtue of who you are or where you're from. Also known as "Privilege."

Advantage Mindset – a set of beliefs about and typical reactions to concepts of advantage defined as "fixed" or "growth," based on the work of Carol Dweck.

Calling out – to "issue a direct challenge to something they've said or done, usually in public and with the intent of exposing the person's wrongdoing to others." Calling in – refers to "the act of checking your peers and getting them to change problematic behavior by explaining their misstep with compassion and patience."[2]

Diversity – the range of human differences across traits of who you are, including gender, race, and sexual identity, along with personality and others; and also, the range of lived experiences where you're from and who you are.

Equity – the consistent and systematic, fair, just, and impartial treatment of all individuals by other individuals and the community.

---

[1] Merriam-Webster, Definition of "advantage," 2022. Available from www.merriam-webster.com/dictionary/advantage [accessed May 3, 2022].

[2] Ashley Austrew, "Is there a difference between 'calling in' and 'calling out'?" *Dictionary.com,* March 22, 2019. Available from www.dictionary.com/e/calling-in-vs-calling-out/ [accessed May 5, 2022].

Headwind – a wind having the opposite general direction to a course of movement (as of an aircraft); a force or influence that slows progress to an improved condition.

Tailwind – a wind having the same general direction as a course of movement (as of an aircraft); a force or influence that advances progress toward an improved condition.

Inclusion – meeting the fundamental human need of belongingness and uniqueness, respecting being part of a community and being an individual, and providing space and opportunity to meet both of those needs.

We also have a Glossary at the end of the book that includes these terms and some others we use. One question we received early in our writing process was about why we say "advantage" if we're talking about "privilege." That question is worth a deeper dive.

"Advantage" rather than "privilege"

Through experience, reviews, interviews, and discussions developing this book, we decided to use "advantage" rather than "privilege." This is not to avoid the word "privilege" as it inevitably comes up and, like any words that come up, is welcome for exploration. But since it's sure to be asked, we want to explain why we're using "advantage" instead of "privilege."

For a host of reasons, we believe that "privilege" calls to mind distinctions of "class" and diminishes perceptions of "effort" that confound these discussions. This is particularly true for those with privilege, and it kicks in before discussion and inquiry even begin. The relative recency of "privilege" in the broader social contexts of social justice and equity, and its nature as unconscious to its owner, similar to unconscious biases, makes the word challenging before even getting to its meaning. Inevitably, those with privilege react to the concept by sharing or holding self-proving examples of "earning" what they have gained. Some with privilege will also react with rationalizations, even if unconsciously held, of how "others" deserve what they have *not* gained or have lost. Those with privilege may also react, whether they realize it or not, with an emotional cycle of guilt/resentment that results in denial or withdrawal – or the occasional eruption.

In our experience, however, "advantage" initiates a more productive response. Advantage seems well understood without as many emotional or social additives as privilege. Further, breaking advantage down into "earned" and "unearned" allows for self-proving examples of "I worked for it" or "No one gave me anything." Allowing these examples allows readers to share their self-validating stories of earned advantage without defensiveness, which typical DEI programs do not generate or may even inhibit or disallow.

"I worked for it, or No one gave me anything."

More importantly, this approach allows the exploration of *unearned* advantages. We've found that when people with advantage can safely share that they have earned (at least some of) what they have, they more easily recognize their unearned advantages. Not only that – allowing a full discussion of earned advantage opens the door to a discussion of the *opportunity* for earned advantage – which comes from effort, relationships, luck – and from *unearned* advantage.

Awareness of privilege, or what we will call unearned advantage, is the usual starting point for many DEI programs and books. The "privilege walk" is an exercise where people standing in a line are prompted to self-identify their unearned advantages and step forward for each one they hold. It is a standard DEI experience designed to raise awareness. Unfortunately, despite its intentions, Robert, like others with privilege, experiences this exercise as shaming rather than illuminating. Ironically, a further challenge with this exercise and DEI programs, in general, is the lack of resourcing to those called out as having privilege, who, if they accept it at all, typically respond with, "What do I do with this?"

> *The irony that people with unearned advantage need to be resourced is not lost on us.*

The irony that people with unearned advantage need to be resourced is not lost on us. That said, without fully enabling the coming to terms of those with unearned advantage, they find it harder to engage. If we cannot engage those with it, at best, they remain on the sidelines, or worse, they retreat further. The inclusion of mindfulness practices in this program supports all participants as they face the inevitable discomforts in it – for those *having* and those *not having* unearned advantage and *the effect* unearned advantage has on the *distribution* of earned advantage opportunities.

Why no "disadvantage"?

As you read, you may wonder, "Why don't they talk about 'disadvantage'? I can think of several of those!" It's a fair question, so we'll explain. Our construct of unearned advantages is that people have them or they don't. In the research behind this book, some felt identifying "disadvantages" would feel supportive to those without advantages instead of simply having few or no advantages. For example, being White in America is an unearned advantage, while being of color in America would be an unearned disadvantage (if you're reacting to this statement, hang with us for a bit). In this example, both "have" something – which can be appealing. So why didn't we do that?

Simply put, applying this to every source of advantage creates a much more complex framework than simply having or not having. It may also generate conflicted feelings unrelated to the evidence about any particular advantage. For example, being a "loud and proud" minority (of any kind) may support a sense of identity, community, motivation, or self-esteem. Still, it doesn't mitigate a particular majority's unearned advantage or "level the playing field" or expand overall earned advantage opportunity – which is our purpose.

Another complication with naming disadvantages would be framing up *unearned disadvantage* with *earned disadvantage*. This would require exploring opportunities lost or consequences levied due to poor behaviors (earned) but would then have to extend into the *conditions* surrounding those behaviors and the root causes of those conditions (often unearned). We focus on what individuals and leaders can do to reduce the impact of unearned advantage and expand opportunities for earned advantage wherever they can. So, we don't deal with disadvantage because we aim to simplify language, allow complexities of feelings without judgment, and facilitate concrete action.

The team

Throughout our story, you'll meet members of a team representing people we have worked with in our careers or been ourselves. As the story unfolds, you'll learn more about each character and, we intend, you'll learn more about yourself. Our characters could be coworkers in an office setting, volunteers in a community organization, or new to each other as members of a team. We will describe them as participating in the first of several DEI sessions organized by a local chambers of commerce. They are tasked with developing public/private partnerships focused on accelerating economic development in communities where our characters have some influence. They haven't worked together much. The story, however, is not about their project or job title but about the individuals, who they are and where they're from, and how they begin to explore the elephant.

Now, you may be a person pushing through this book who is saying to yourself: "Well, what do these characters have to do with me? I am not a person with a big title or a lot of power!" Our response is: Get ready to discover just how much you can be a key player wherever you contribute to a team. We'll explore scenarios later on. What's important for you to know from the start is that people like you make or break progress. In fact, our experience is that people like you often inspire, inform, and influence the people who do have big titles and power. When there are significant numbers of people within an organization or community with shared intentions toward growing advantage, your influence often can be hard to ignore.

You will learn more about our characters along the way, but here's what they learned about each other in their first meeting:

Robert – a long-serving senior manager on the team respected for his experience and knowledge. Robert identifies himself as a White, middle-aged male. He is married to a woman with whom he's raising a family.

Maria – an experienced marketer with an impressive resume. A 30-something with light-colored hair and skin, Maria identifies herself as a Latina who emigrated from South America with her family in her school-age years.

Yvonne – a highly competent communications manager with a background in business and nonprofit organizations. Yvonne identifies herself as an African-American woman who put herself through college and graduate school while working.

Alvin – a younger, successful, innovative technology whiz, Alvin is athletic and new to the area. He identifies himself as an American-Asian male with strong ties to his Chinese parents, who built their own business to ensure Alvin's education.

All of these characters are composites, and each is, as you will find, much more than described here. Of course, with the nearly infinite number of possible intersections of who you are and where you're from, we're missing so many that we can't describe them all. That said, we're trusting you will see something you recognize along the way. If you think one of our characters is you or someone you know, that's a coincidence. But if the shoe fits…

Chapter 1: Recognizing advantage

Through the eyes of...

Alvin

Alvin was reflecting on his seminar experience and some of the programs he'd attended in the past. "I get the 'male privilege' thing. When my parents lived in China, every parent hoped for a boy, and it didn't change much from there. Of course, it's not like that here, but I'm pretty sure guys got called on before girls by teachers in my schools – even by women teachers!

Then there's the whole 'Tiger child' thing because my family is from Asia, and people assume I work harder (OK, I do) or am better at science (Tech yes, Biology, please no!) than others. But just because I'm Asian? I know Asians who don't work harder and aren't science savants – and I know White and Black people who do and are!

My parents worked hard, so I got to live in a decent neighborhood – clean water, clean streets, good grocery stores, and pretty good schools! I got to take lessons in two languages and played on the school tennis team and some other sports – I'm fortunate to be able to try almost anything I want to. And where I grew up, there was no crime." He thought for a moment, "No crime until my dad got pushed down for 'bringing the coronavirus here,' according to some jerk."

"It would be nice to tell my colleagues that I'm gay, but I get the feeling they'd rather we 'Don't ask' and 'Don't tell' that whole thing. My LGBTQ friends agree – it would be easier to be straight in this world and stop feeling like I have to keep explaining the acronym! But that's NOT something I talk to others about. Aside from that, I guess I do have some advantages that some other people don't. Like Yvonne – I feel sorry for her!"

Yvonne

Yvonne, however, doesn't feel sorry for herself. "I got scholarships and financial aid to pay for college – the first of my family to graduate! I grew up in a poorer neighborhood than most people I work with. We had lead-tainted water and two lousy choices for grocery shopping in walking or bus distance. And don't talk to me about crime in the neighborhood – talk to me about why young men I knew were locked up for minor drug charges, changing their lives forever, when other young men outside my neighborhood weren't. Male privilege? Not in my community!

I am inspired every day when I see people like me – from all races and backgrounds – overcoming obstacles like I did and helping to bring up others. But I also have to work hard every day to be optimistic because I am so tired of seeing the same show play on life's TV.

A Black man is killed by some blue police, some White racist, or some Black criminal, and too many people in the world who are willfully ignorant of historical, persistent, deep inequality of opportunity toward whole population groups react with shock or worse, blame, toward the murdered Black man.

My sister has a son – my nephew. She is scared to death to let him go out – day or night. My mother raised me to be self-sufficient, and she succeeded – my sister is trying to do the same thing – but it seems like it's harder today.

As I think about my career, I know I've gotten some opportunities from different people – men and women of all colors. It annoys me that some people think – heck, even said! – that I got those because I am Black or a woman, or I 'checked off two boxes for one.' Aside from the insult, my performance shows that's just not true. I am talented – it just seems I have to do twice as much to prove it. I wonder if Maria feels like that?"

Maria

Maria feels some of that. "It's not always easy being a woman in business. I don't often get the feeling eyes are undressing me, but it happens. More often, I'm the one expected to organize the meetings – one guy keeps asking me to organize lunch! But I know I have had advantages – being a Latina passing for White is one – 'colorizing' they call it? I guess the 'advantage' is the passing for White part! It's a little weird for me – whether here or back home in Venezuela, I have an advantage over indigenous and darker-colored people – but I don't feel like I'm White! Either place, I do not entirely feel like I'm home – that doesn't seem like an advantage.

I was able to attend the best schools both in Venezuela and in the U.S. – pretty lucky! From those and my family's friends, I made connections and got mentors who have helped me get opportunities that others didn't have access to. I have made the most of those – no one would put me forward if they felt I would embarrass them!

Where I live now has plenty of Latin American immigrants. My church community is huge – I guess it's the dominant religion in the area. We don't discriminate against others, but it seems we keep attracting people like ourselves – so it's a strong community! I love living here – but I wouldn't expect to see Robert moving in any time soon."

Robert

"Let's see, I'm male, college-educated, straight, White, able-bodied, Christian-raised, English-only language." He paused, "Oh yes, I'm an extrovert! If only I were 2" taller...," he mused. Robert had heard and understood the message in the seminar – but was annoyed, to put it mildly. "Man, was I PISSED! In the privilege walk exercise, I ended up at the front of the line. That was SO embarrassing! It was a complete setup. It's not my fault how I was born or that I grew up in safe, healthy neighborhoods with good schools."

"After the program, I asked the facilitator, 'What am I supposed to DO with this newfound knowledge of my privilege?' Do you know what she said? She said, 'Just be aware of it.' Really? Here I am brought to the end of my road of ignorance, and you won't give me at least an idea of where I can go from here?"

Each and all of us have the choice to look at and recognize advantage as the elephant in the room that it is. Of course, recognizing isn't easy – but you must start somewhere.

Recognizing advantage – what am I looking at?

The parable of the blindfolded wise sages and the elephant goes back to about 500 BCE and still resonates in story-telling and literature today (many versions are available on the internet). Each sage, blindfolded (literally or figuratively, by force or by choice), meets and knows one part of the elephant and declares it to represent the entire elephant.

As the picture below and common sense make clear, that can't be right. The moral of the story is that people tend to claim absolute truth based on their limited, subjective experience while ignoring or denying the limited, subjective truth of others. It's not that any one of them is entirely wrong; it's just that none of them is completely right.

Image credit: Maria Laura Garza

It's not that any one of them is entirely wrong; it's just that none of them is completely right.

The elephant parable plays out in everyday life in many ways. We're human – we see what we see and know what we know. The problem is – we don't see what we won't look at, and we can't know what we won't think about. That some people have unearned advantages others don't (and can't) have is one of the most enormous elephants in the room today. But it IS in the room. Unfortunately, none of us has a full view of it, and most of us are afraid if we get close, we'll get trumpeted from the trunk, stepped on by a leg, gored by a tusk, or whipped by a tail!

One part of the elephant that most of us *do* recognize is that there are many kinds of *earned advantages* in life that are available, to some degree, to everyone. So, *recognizing* advantage begins with understanding sources of advantage, beginning with sources of earned advantage.

Recognizing earned advantage

Earned advantages are benefits or positions gained or granted by virtue of what you do without regard to how you're born or where you're raised. So, when Robert exclaimed, "I've earned what I have!" he was thinking of examples of earned advantage. That's also true of Yvonne, Alvin, and Maria. There are many sources of earned advantage, but in general, they are benefits earned through your sources of effort, commitment, and diligence. Other sources are the development and application of natural talents and skills, for example, Robert's insight and influencing skills, Yvonne's perseverance and learning agility, and Alvin's technical prowess.

Another attribute of earned advantages is that they are granted to you through your effort, etc., or by others in response to it. For example, Maria has opportunities from her network of sponsors and mentors. Close working relationships contribute to opportunities, promotions, and recognition. Sources of earned advantage have some difficulty to earn, ranging from taking a class, learning a language, earning a degree, or consistently performing well in a job, or managing a life-change choice, like migrating countries for more opportunity. Yvonne's academic achievements or Alvin's talent for technology or Maria's family migrations are sources of earned advantage.

An earned advantage has a simple test to pass – it is an advantage obtainable through your effort without regard to who you were born as or where you grew up. From the examples given, you can develop a list of earned advantages. This is a good moment to reflect and do that for yourself.

Earned advantage exercise

Take a moment to step back from what you have read so far. Allow any clarifying questions about what you've read to settle to the bottom of your mind.

As you reflect on these examples of earned advantage, list your own sources of earned advantage. Check to see if they were gained without regard to who you are or where you're from.

If they were, consider this question: was the opportunity to pursue each earned advantage equally available to all without regard to who they are or where they were raised? Allow this question to sink in before answering.

As you consider this question, see if you are staying close to a part of the elephant you already know to avoid another part representing someone else's uncomfortable reality. Are you worried about being trumpeted, stepped on, or gored?

Are you answering based on how you believe things should be in anyone's experience or how they actually are in the experience of other people?

Even if you are unsure how to answer the question above, how would you describe your feelings when you ponder the question? (Noting these feelings may help you later on as you continue making sense of things and eventually deciding how, if at all, you wish to grow your mindset.)

After considering that question, take a moment and mentally step back from the answers that came up. Take a moment for a deep, slow breath in and out.

Reflections of this kind often yield an unpleasant truth – while everyone has sources of earned advantages, the opportunity to gain them is not equitably distributed. Why is that? It's another part of the elephant of advantage called unearned advantage.

The unearned opportunities for earned advantage – unearned advantage

Unearned advantages are the benefits or positions gained or granted by virtue of *who you are* or *where you're from*. "Who you are" includes things about you that are true from birth. "Where you're from" includes things that affected you from that moment onward. Some of these things bring or don't bring certain advantages that help or hurt the opportunity to progress. So, before we differentiate between who you are and where you're from, let's differentiate helps from hurts – tailwinds and headwinds.

Image credit: Maria Laura Garza

Headwind – a wind having the opposite general direction to a course of movement (as of an aircraft); a force or influence that slows progress to an improved condition.

Tailwind – a wind having the same general direction as a course of movement (as of an aircraft); a force or influence that advances progress toward an improved condition.[1]

If you've ever flown a long distance, especially along an east–west longitude, you'll have noticed it often takes longer to travel in one direction than the other. It's not just the time-change; it's due to headwinds and tailwinds. If you're a pilot and managing fuel consumption, you have to accept it will take longer to get to your destination or that you'll have to carry and use more fuel to get there than another plane that isn't facing those headwinds. So, you can get there – but it takes either more time or more fuel. And you are quite aware of these headwinds hitting you right in your face each mile of the flight!

Another pilot is flying with tailwinds. This pilot can fly with less effort or get to the destination faster – or both – than the one facing headwinds. Like headwinds, tailwinds can be light or heavy and can take a little or a lot of the load. However, as drivers, runners, and pilots can tell you, an interesting thing about tailwinds is that you aren't as aware of tailwinds because they aren't hitting you in the face. You may suspect

---

[1] Merriam-Webster, Definitions of "headwind" and "tailwind," 2022. Available from www.merriam-webster.com/dictionary/headwind and www.merriam-webster.com/dictionary/tailwind [accessed May 3, 2022].

they are behind you, but you don't often notice. Or, and often, you don't suspect them and chalk up their influence to your personal effort or luck.

And just as people touching a part of the elephant know their part and not others', we notice our own experiences before noticing those of others, if we notice their experiences at all.

Having and not having unearned advantages is just like facing headwinds and tailwinds. We don't notice tailwinds that help us and don't always see headwinds that impede others because our tailwinds are always at our backs and their headwinds are always in their faces. Because headwinds begin at birth, even those facing them may stop recognizing them or may accept them as "the way it is." By their nature, unearned advantages are, in fact, "the way it is" because they are generally (with some exceptions) not things we can change. What are these things?

Sources of unearned advantages

Like it or not – and many don't – there is plenty of research and science that makes clear that, in aggregate, people with certain traits face challenges that people with other traits don't. This is true globally and locally and is related to the basic human tendency to prefer similar company. If you're wondering or skeptical about this, you could explore the research of others, some of which we list in the Additional Reading section, or simply take a moment and reflect for yourself.

Who we are exercise

Take a moment to settle yourself in a comfortable but alert position – perhaps sitting with feet on the floor, hands in lap, and with as erect a spine as is comfort-able. Practice the breath exercise we introduced at the end of the Introduction. Give yourself a minute.

Recall or imagine walking into a meeting room, cafe-teria, or another place where people gather. Each table has an open seat. Recognizing we rarely think about this consciously, consider this question, "What influences where you choose to sit?"

After thinking about this, consider this question, "What really influences where you choose to sit?" Allow yourself to explore your answers.

Take another breath, perhaps this time allowing a fuller exhalation than the first time.

Notice if you sense any emotional reactions to these questions and your answers. Do you find yourself annoyed, defensive, validated, or a bit uncertain? See if you can observe your reaction as if it were removed from you. Breathe again.

It's natural to judge our own responses to this kind of question, "Of course I do this..." "I would never do that..." "Um, I guess I do this...." "I don't know what I do!" and "Can I think of something else, now, please!?" Whichever response or responses you had, take a moment and pause between the answer and your explanation or justification for it.

This simple exercise generates a full spectrum of reac-tions and responses – whatever you feel is what you feel

– it's OK. Awareness of sources of unearned advantage comes harder to those who have them, as we saw with Robert. On the other hand, repeated experiences by those without them can be exhausting, as we saw with Yvonne, or conflicting as we saw with Maria, or cause anxiety about others' reactions, as with Alvin. And there are more sources than you might think!

Unearned advantage – who you are

Many sources of unearned advantage are genetic and include innate traits like gender, sexual orientation, identity, race, ethnicity, and ability/disability. Dominant cultures also provide sources of unearned advantage from histories of government policy, law, and other informal practices established by whoever has been or is "in charge." Dominant cultures can be the majority in number or a minority holding accumulated power and wealth.

Other culturally influenced sources of unearned advantage include trait perceptions of attractiveness, height, body type, hair, skin color, and various personality traits. As we saw with Maria, her experience as a light-colored Latina seemed different to her – advantaged – than that of darker-colored Latinas. Maria was beginning to work through her sense of how things *should be* compared to how they *actually are* for people different from herself.

Robert had a similar insight after sharing his experience with his brother. "If I were just taller, I'd have it all," Robert had said. His brother, a bit shorter in height, took a moment and then replied, "I know you're making a joke, dude, but you *do* realize that being 5'10" rather than 5'4" has worked for you, right? I mean, we're the same in every other way, but that difference has made a difference!"

Age is another culturally influenced source of unearned advantage with fascinating – and often conflicting – dynamics.

"What's wrong with young people today?" is hardly a new phrase and yet age discrimination, or "ageism," in the workplace is very real.[2] Younger people, like Alvin, face questions and doubts about loyalty, work ethic, and willingness to sacrifice. Older people, like Robert, face questions and doubts about innovation, flexibility, and willingness to learn. Exactly who is younger and who is older is, of course, in the eye of the beholder. Alvin considers the recent college graduate to be younger, Robert considers Alvin to be younger, and Robert's mom still sees him as a kid (of course, she does).

Ageism is compounded by intersections with other sources of unearned advantage. Research shows that both older women and older African-Americans face headwinds of less access to training[3] and less upward mobility.[4] Both Maria and Yvonne will inevitably face these headwinds and more so than Robert and Alvin. Further complicating all this, the perceptions that drive these realities aren't held just by opposites – people often hold negative stereotypes about others just like themselves. And of course, if you're not ageing, you're not reading this book – so it happens to all of us.

Finally, in terms of who you are, while we don't explore personality much in this book, it's worth noting that certain

[2] Sharon Raj, "Ageism in the workplace – the privilege of being the 'right age.'" *LSE Business Review*, February 3, 2022. Available from https://blogs.lse.ac.uk/businessreview/2022/02/03/ageism-in-the-workplace-the-privilege-of-being-the-right-age/ [accessed May 5, 2022].

[3] George Wilson and Vincent J. Roscigno, "Race, ageism and the slide from privileged occupations." *Social Science Research*, 2018;69: 52–64. https://doi.org/10.1016/j.ssresearch.2017.09.009

[4] Jelle Lössbroek and Jonas Radl (2019), "Teaching older workers new tricks: Workplace practices and gender training differences in nine European countries." *Ageing and Society*, 2019;39(10): 2170–2193. https://doi.org/10.1017/s0144686x1800079x

innate, behavioral traits related to personality are appreciated or tolerated more than others depending on the dominant culture. Certain behavior patterns are considered "disordered" in some cultures but normal – or even valued – in others. The degrees to which people are appreciated for being humble or bold, flamboyant or reserved, and agreeable or contrary (to name a few) varies by what's expected in the community in which you live. While personality is largely innate, the differences in how different behavior patterns are perceived and valued relate to where they are observed – where you're from.

Where you're from

In addition to who you are at birth, where you're from has many sources of unearned advantage. One example is born citizenship. The history of the world is mainly defined by people moving or being moved, by choice, by need, or by force, from one place to another in search of, or taking, advantage. Where you are raised has a lot to do with your access to quality public education, living in a prosperous community, living in a safe neighborhood, and access to essential resources such as clean water, healthy foods, or clean air. Your first or native language is also a source of unearned advantage, as is access to multilingual development. These can be different between countries or between neighborhoods. These are all sources of unearned advantage.

Other sources of where-you're-from advantage include access to or inclusion in community organizations and associations. For example, Maria and her family, practicing Roman Catholics, participate in the parish Knights of Columbus chapter, where they interact with various influential people. She also lives in a thriving, predominantly Hispanic, community whose members dominate local politics and education. Robert has a similar experience – though his upbringing, community, friends, and associations are almost entirely White. These sources of where-you're-from advantage are increasingly described as "social capital,"[5] which is, basically, the idea that social relationships are resources that can contribute to the accumulation of highly valued and rewarded skills and credentials.

Alvin, on the other hand, is new to the area and has found fewer Asian folk and very few Chinese-Americans. "I was raised on the west coast where there were a lot of people who looked like me. Here, I'm a minority, so it doesn't surprise me to BE in the minority," he said. "But it's hard work to fit in and not be the 'Asian guy.'"

Yvonne knows her mother was proud to see her succeed in school and professionally and make a home in a safe neighborhood – even if it's mostly White. "I have Black friends who live closer to each other – but that's not an option for us. Most people are nice – but it would also be nice to share more experiences with people like us."

Pain is inevitable, suffering is optional

It seems like each of our team is making do with what they have. Some people do indeed "rise above" not having all the possible unearned advantages. They fly into the headwinds and still get to their destination, while those with these unearned advantages continue to get there faster or with less effort due to tailwinds. Those without tailwinds will continue to have to work harder or be more talented to get to the same place. Accepting this as "the way it is" will not change it. So, the question is, how is it changed?

---

[5] Richard Machalek and Michael W. Martin, "Sociobiology and sociology: A new synthesis," in International Encyclopedia of the Social & Behavioral Sciences (Second Edition). Elsevier, 2015.

There is an old saying, associated with eastern philosophies but commonly heard in the west, "Pain is inevitable, suffering is optional." Another way of saying this, coined by our team when facing a seemingly impossible task, was, "It is what it is, but it will be what we make it." Recognizing that headwinds and tailwinds are inevitable doesn't mean they can't be buffered or shared. While many people with less advantage do optimize their contributions, it's through sheer determination. The opportunity for intentional diversity, equity, and inclusion is to grow the elephant of earned advantage *for everyone*, which generates benefits *for everyone*. Another important goal of intentional DEI is doing what we can – from wherever we sit on our teams or in our communities – to optimize the contributions of everyone, to help everyone contribute their best, to do more than survive but to thrive. Accepting "the way it is" without intention to change it means we accept less than the best in innovation, collaboration, and problem-solving. In an increasingly interconnected world, choosing to accept "the way it is" fails in the self, in the marketplace, and in the community.

"But what am I supposed to do about my unearned advantages?!" Robert had asked. "It's not like I can give them BACK!"

The point of recognizing sources of unearned advantage is not to "give them back." You can't give back who you were born as or where you were raised. While it's possible to change personality, appearance, and even the body, attributes of who you are and where you're from are, for the most part, what they are. The question is, whoever you are and wherever you're from, can you see the entire elephant – Earned and Unearned? Can you see unearned advantages for what they are, who has them, without emotional judgment, so together we can reduce their influence and expand the sources, the opportunity, for earned advantage for everyone?

STOP – begin to see the elephant

S Stop

T Take a breath

O Observe

P Proceed

Image credit: Maria Laura Garza

These questions can be challenging to explore. And while a child might have an easier time seeing the entire elephant at once because they haven't "learned" not to, it's hard for adults to set their eyes on it without wanting to look away. So, it can help to have a simple way to take that breath as you did at the end of the Introduction when you need it.

Before the infamous DEI seminar, Maria had completed an eight-week stress-management program called Mindfulness-Based Stress Reduction (MBSR) to help her more effectively respond to stressors she was facing at home. "I remember one of the skills we learned was how to STOP when we felt ourselves reacting instead of responding to something stressful. I think that might help me make sense of what I'm feeling about advantage." Here's what she learned.

S – stands for "Stop." Stop what you're doing and pause, assuming you're not driving a car or operating machinery! Put things down for a moment, including uncomfortable thoughts about who has advantage and who doesn't, and why that's not fair or not true or anything else about it. "My mind kept swirling around whether I have unearned advantage or not," Maria said. "Part of me said it didn't matter, and part did. I needed to pause for a moment just to see what question I wanted to ask myself."

T – stands for "Taking a full, slow breath." Maria practiced using the expansive breath technique you learned earlier – and so can you. Or just take a moment and notice how you are breathing. You may or may not be breathing differently from usual, or perhaps breathing faster and more shallowly or with big breaths or even sighs. In the words of author and mindfulness teacher Jon Kabat-Zinn, "As long as you're breathing, there's more right with you than wrong with you." The T in STOP prompts you to breathe and creates the opportunity for O – Observe.

O – stands for "Observe." Observe your experience just as it is – including thoughts, feelings, and emotions. When you practice Observe, you can see what's going on without automatically reacting to it. Maria reflected, and so can you, that thoughts about advantage are not necessarily facts, and they are not permanent. Instead, you can observe any emotions present and how they're being expressed in the body in that moment. Maria learned that just naming her feelings, including being conflicted, can turn the volume down on that part of her brain and have a calming effect. Then she noticed her body – was she tense, rigid, standing, or sitting? She caught her posture and expressions and, in a mirror, she realized what her family meant when they said, "Maria, chill out!"

P – stands for "Proceed." Proceed with an intention for what and how you choose to respond to what's happening. Maria laughed, "Well, sometimes I 'proceed' by excusing myself to get a glass of water to settle my thoughts before returning, and sometimes I settle in for a solid debate because I'm ready to go!" Maria had learned that STOP didn't mean she was to stop without going again. She realized that, sometimes, you STOP so you *can* go again.

Recognizing the entire elephant

Recognizing earned and unearned advantage is hard and necessary – but insufficient. Recognizing *the relationship* between them is essential. As you've seen in our teams' experiences, some face headwinds, and some benefit from tailwinds. It gets complicated to convert "headwinds" into "disadvantages," so we say you have certain unearned advantages or you don't. The more unearned advantages you have, the greater your odds of success at the same effort or at the same time as others. The fewer you have, the lower your odds of success at the same effort or at the same time as others.

Advantage and opportunities

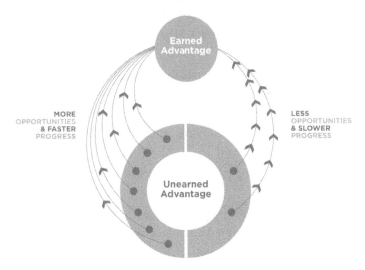

Image credit: Maria Laura Garza

This model shows the uneven distribution of unearned advantage and how it relates to earned advantage. Overall, in our team, Robert has more unearned advantages, "If I were only two inches taller..." he had said. As uncomfortable as it made Robert feel, he recognizes that White, heterosexual, able-bodied, English-only speaking men have advantages from the crib (English-only speakers require *others* to learn English, "the language of business"). In terms of advantages, he has one more than his wife. She is similar to him in every way except her gender. He also has one more than his son – who is similar to him in every way except his son has a physical disability. So, yes, if Robert were over 6' tall, he'd truly have every available unearned advantage of who you are.

On top of these, Robert has unearned advantages due to where he's from. He grew up and was educated in an environment superior to most people *in the history of the entire planet*! Good schools, intact family, safe environment, etc., Robert truly has more unearned advantage than most people different from him.

Does this mean Robert or those like him have not gained earned advantages by their own effort? *No, it does not mean that.*

Having unearned advantages is no guarantee of gaining earned advantages. You can probably think of some people who "had it all" and wasted it with poor choices or lack of effort. However, what having unearned advantages *does* mean is that Robert and those like him had *more opportunities* to make *faster progress* than those without their unearned advantages.

Yvonne, Maria, and other women, regardless of color, face the reality that women earn less money than men for the same work and get fewer opportunities for senior jobs. Being paid less is unfair, and it limits options for career growth. Some critics poke at these facts with rationales of maternity leave and "mommy track" careers. However, these critics miss an obvious point – it compares wages for the same jobs. Opportunities for job assignments, leadership roles, and perceptions of "fit" are also influenced by gender. Another established reality is that people of color, particularly women of color, are substantially underrepresented in leadership positions – of any kind. The rationales explaining these facts, those not related to unearned advantage, reflect a serious lack of data, perspective, and insight.

In Alvin's case, sharing that he is gay creates risk if someone with influence over his career is not open-minded about sexual orientation. *Should it* be that biases against LGBTQ people *never* influence their careers? Let's agree it should. But *is that true?* That would be nice, but no, it's not. So, is it any wonder why Alvin or others are willing to "be in the closet" and deny or cover that part of their identity? Does Alvin risk being skipped over until he knows those making decisions are free of biases? Will he ever know that?

Recognizing the entire elephant of advantage is disconcerting whether you have many or few sources of unearned advantage. The recognition of *having them* often stimulates reactions of unresolvable guilt and defensiveness that result in wanting to rationalize, defend, or deny them. At the same time, the recognition of *not having them* often stimulates reactions of resentment, anger, or exhaustion that result in being torn between wanting to fight back somehow or toss in the towel and surrender.

We said this wasn't going to be easy. The elephant is here. But if you're still holding on to part of it, here's an opportunity for a break.

The discomfort of recognizing unearned advantage

"Is it hot in here, or is it just me?"

The authors, and just about everyone else...

We've introduced some breathing and reflection practices intended to help you slow the heart rate and breathing and turn a little more toward the less-comfortable truths about unearned advantage. Whether you have many or few, just talking about it is stressful. We've adapted a positive and powerful practice that can help you sit with what's present from author, lawyer, and mindfulness expert Rhonda Magee in her book, *The Inner Work of Racial Justice.*[6] Take a moment and experiment with this awareness of advantage practice. You can also experiment with this in the audio recordings available on the book website www.growingtheelephant.com

Awareness of advantage – reflection

Take a moment to settle yourself in a comfortable but alert position – perhaps sitting with feet on the floor, hands in lap, and with as erect a spine as is comfortable. Practice the breath exercise we introduced at the end of Chapter 1. Give yourself a minute.

What thoughts, emotions, and sensations come up when you are asked to turn toward the topic of

---

[6] Rhonda Magee, *The Inner Work of Racial Justice: Healing Ourselves and Transforming Our Communities Through Mindfulness.* TarcherPerigree, 2019.

sources of unearned advantage when you are alone? What comes up when you are in the company of others like you? What comes up when you are in a mixed company?

What are some of the stories you tell yourself to explain the differences in why certain people have more or fewer opportunities for earned advantage? Do these stories reflect how you believe the world should be or how the world actually is in the experience of others?

What insights on unearned and earned advantage are you aware of now that you may not have been aware of before reading and reflecting?

Now, allow yourself to release the thoughts, emotions, and sensations that arose as you considered these questions. Allow that these experiences are natural and human – just like you.

In the Introduction, you read about the zones of comfort, growth, and overwhelm. At that point, you might have wondered, "What could possibly be overwhelming in this book?" In this chapter, you may have found *recognizing* unearned advantage as challenging as our team found it. Depending on your experience, you may have experienced *growth* or perhaps a sense of *overwhelm*. Continuously experiencing a sense of overwhelm, whether it's a lived experience of harm or threat or an experience of constant fear of loss, creates the potential for traumatic stress. Whether you are feeling this or not, it's important to realize that many do and will.

A brief introduction to windows of tolerance

Sometimes, recognizing unearned advantage, or any difficult subject for that matter, surfaces intense feelings, sensations, or thoughts from our own experience or those of others. Depending on who you are and where you're from, these experiences can range from the mildly annoying to the genuinely traumatic. We can't do justice to dealing with traumatic and post-traumatic stress in this book. Still, we must cast some light on the subject since it's inevitable that some readers will have experienced traumatic stress related to the unequal experiences of unearned advantages – including both those with advantages and those without them.

Developed by UCLA Professor of Psychiatry Dan Siegel, MD and furthered by Stephen Porges, Ph.D., and David Treleaven, the "window of tolerance" is that optimal, middle-zone of normal functionality between being overly energized (hyper-arousal) and under-energized (hypo-arousal).[7] We all can get "knocked out" of our window by an event or perception – all humans do. This is something to be aware of, especially as you explore advantage. Being aware that you can come out of your window can help you return to it if that happens.

---

[7] National Institute for the Clinical Application of Behavioral Medicine, "How to help your clients understand their window of tolerance," 2019. Available from www.nicabm.com/trauma-how-to-help-your-clients-understand-their-window-of-tolerance/ [accessed May 5, 2022].

As you *recognize* unearned advantage, whether you have a lot or a little, you may notice different sensations as you recall memories, reflect on current events, or imagine future situations. You may notice sensations similar to experiencing stress even if you're unsure of what is stressing you. You may recall or contemplate a particularly painful experience that feels like it's happening right now. Intense, lasting feelings of resentment, fear, or anger, particularly when left unaddressed or cultivated, can be as debilitating as physical injury.

When someone fears their opportunity to survive and thrive will not be given or will be taken away, the mind and body react in a stress response. If the stress response isn't managed properly, it can lead to anxiety and, taken far or long enough, to traumatic stress.

While we live in times and cultures where an individual's ability to dominate difficulty is highly valued and admitting to being stressed is not, the reality is that negative emotions and stress are at a global high and individuals are not equipped to manage it.[8] These realities are in no small part due to the challenges of recognizing unearned advantage – and facing these realities can bring you out of your window. Being deeply or often out of your window can result in hyper-arousal – anxious, angry, out of control, overwhelmed, or hypo-arousal – spacy, zoned out, numbed, frozen. In either case, you didn't plan to feel this way, you just do.

When you notice any of this, consider taking a break and resource yourself as you best know how – water, breath, movement, a friend, or just time away. In our story, Maria found practices of meditation and movement helped her, while Alvin found release in sports activities. If you find any negative feelings linger beyond a few days, consider speaking with a trusted counselor. For more information, particularly for those guiding these discussions, we highly recommend reading up on windows of tolerance at the National Institute for the Clinical Application of Behavioral Medicine (nicabm.com) and David Treleaven's book *Trauma-Sensitive Mindfulness*.[9]

---

[8] Gallup, *Gallup Global Emotions*, 2021. Available from www.gallup.com/analytics/349280/gallup-global-emotions-report.aspx [accessed May 5, 2022].

[9] David Treleaven, *Trauma-Sensitive Mindfulness: Practices for Safe and Transformative Healing*. W. W. Norton, 2018.

Chapter summary

In this chapter, you focused on recognizing advantage, the elephant in the room. You learned more about the team and, perhaps, gained insight into yourself. You explored the sources and opportunities for earned advantage, the uncomfortable realities of unearned advantages, and the relationship they have. You felt a few or many of the headwinds you face, recognized a few that others face, and became more aware of tailwinds, as well. You learned you can STOP when the going gets tough so that you can go again and, if the going gets too tough, to resource yourself toward your window of tolerance.

By recognizing and staying present with both earned and unearned advantage, whether you have a little or a lot, you may be better able to separate how things should be from how they are in your own experience and the experience of others. Like any other new knowledge or awareness, you will expand and refine it each time you explore it.

At different points, your exploration may become annoying, concerning, or even distressing. At points, you may, like both Robert and Yvonne, become frustrated with "how it is" and want to ignore, deny, or surrender to what seems an insurmountable challenge. If this occurs, take heart and know that you grow opportunities for earned advantage on the scale that matters the most – your own. You have to work with the elephant before you can grow it.

Recognizing advantage – reflection

As you have read about our team and their stories, what resonated with you in your experience?

What about the experiences of other people has occurred to you? Imagine how people you know who are similar to who you are or where you're from have reacted to parts of this chapter.

Imagine how people you know who are different from who you are or where you're from have reacted to parts of this chapter.

Without imagining what you might "do" differently going forward, what have you learned about recognizing sources of earned and unearned advantage? What do you suppose will be easier and more difficult to work with moving ahead?

Chapter 2: Working with advantage – the mindset

Recognizing advantage, particularly unearned advantage, is not easy and the more you have, the harder it is. However, once you see it, it's hard to un-see it unless you close your eyes or walk away. So, being one who chooses not to un-see it, you can begin to work with it. This is where mindset comes in.

Continuing to look into yourself is like touching a different part of the elephant – it takes courage. If you're familiar with the trunk, you may want to avoid the legs. If you know the legs, you may want to avoid the tail. There's no perfect or "right" way to take hold of any particular part. When we do, especially at first, we almost always grab too hard or pinch accidentally or get a knee-jerk reaction. Remember, an elephant (and advantage) is a living thing, after all. Working with advantage is like that.

As we muster up the courage to touch different parts and get comfortable with the occasionally uncomfortable reaction we get from reaching out, we all grow. We're afraid of being trumpeted, stepped on, gored, whipped, etc. – that's being human. But exploring the discomforts of *recognizing* unearned advantage is necessary to begin *working with* it. The more we do, the better we get. Mindset helps.

The team explores Advantage Mindset – fixed or growth?

In another seminar, years before, Robert had learned about "growth mindset." Simply put, in a growth mindset, people believe they can develop their abilities and talents if they work at it and are willing to try, fail, and learn. Pioneered by Carol Dweck in her best-selling book, *Mindset*,[1] and since adapted for use in education, business, and science, growth mindset is compared to a "fixed mindset" where things "are what they are" and are hard or impossible to change. Robert had prided himself on having a growth mindset when learning new skills or adapting to new situations.

> *Simply put, in a growth mindset, people believe they can develop their abilities and talents if they work at it and are willing to try, fail, and learn.*

---

[1] Carol Dweck, *Mindset: The New Psychology of Success*. Random House, 2006.

But "I wonder," he said, "if I have a growth or fixed mindset when it comes to advantage? Let me be honest with myself. Do I truly believe spending my precious time thinking about these issues is going to change how I think or act in a way that makes a difference in my life or career?"

As it turned out, Robert wasn't the only team member familiar with Dweck's groundbreaking work. Each had been in seminars or read one of the many books or watched one of the internet videos explaining and expanding growth mindset. Just as Robert had found, however, adapting growth mindset to advantage involved exploring and questioning some embedded assumptions.

Alvin wondered how he might grow his current mindset about older people and technology. "Is it really possible for me to believe people who are more than a decade older than me could actually problem-solve as well as I do on tech issues? There's a lot of value in experience and I don't have that much. But in my experience, experience isn't wisdom and sometimes it just slows things down. Since that's my lived experience, how am I ever going to learn to think differently any time soon?"

Maria wondered if she ever could dispel her belief that a person who did not receive elite education could be in any way a stronger, more effective leader than she is at her organization. "True, I have been in a few situations where one particular office mate regularly comes up with product ideas that I never even thought about. I always assumed it was because he grew up in neighborhoods like many of our customers. But now, I'm wondering if I need to work on thinking differently. Maybe I should have been asking for his insights about strategy and marketing tactics too!"

After the less-than-successful DEI seminar, the team decided to explore mindset as a reading group and see what they could apply to working with advantage.

In their discussions, they realized that, while unearned advantages were not changeable, how people thought about them was. "It's like what I learned in MBSR class," said Maria, referring again to her training in stress reduction. "While I can't change what happens to me, I can change how I respond to it!" Once the team recognized unearned advantage, they realized they have choices about what they believe about it – which could change its impact on opportunity for earned advantage.

The Growth Advantage Mindset – GAM

Your mindset, or established set of attitudes, begins with your natural traits but develops over time based on life experiences. Your mindset is a lens through which you see and understand the world – it interprets and decodes everything you perceive, so it's quite powerful! Here are a few important points about mindset:

1. It does not define you – you are not what you think. You may hold a fixed mindset on a particular topic, but that's something you hold, not something you are.
2. It can be maintained by habit, influenced by events, and changed by choice. A particular mindset can go unchallenged for a lifetime, or can be rocked by an experience, or can be grown by intentional action.
3. It is not uniformly fixed or growth about *everything*. You can hold a growth mindset about your ability to dance while holding a fixed mindset about your ability to speak publicly. You can hold a growth mindset about your potential for success while holding a fixed mindset about the potential of others – and vice-versa.

Psychologist and author Dr. Wendy Ulrich has been studying and working with growth mindset for many years and provides additional insight into these points. "While we all do hold different mindsets on different topics, it's worth noting that the intentional growth of mindset in one area seeps into other areas." She adds:

When you realize you are not your mindset, you give yourself permission to examine it objectively for what it is. When you examine it, you give yourself permission to recognize the experiences in your life that have influenced it, and, critically, that you're capable of intentional action to grow your mindset. When you take that intentional action and grow your mindset – on dancing, on speaking, or on expanding earned advantage – that growth stimulates growth in other areas, as well.[2]

The power of developing a Growth Advantage Mindset is, we hope, also pretty clear – and also not always easy. Many things influence Advantage Mindset: personality, upbringing, culture, experiences – pretty much all of who you are and where you're from. For the most part, we're not aware of the impact it has on us until we work with it.

In this chapter, we introduce an Advantage Mindset framework that may help you differentiate a Fixed Advantage Mindset (FAM) from a Growth Advantage Mindset (GAM). We believe that working with the Advantage Mindset – exploring this part of the elephant – is key to growing earned advantage. At its heart, Dweck's growth mindset is not hard to understand. It is about potential and possibility from intentional effort, learning from the effort, and improving from the learning. The opposite, fixed mindset, is also not hard to understand – don't try, don't learn, don't improve. If you

---

[2] Interview, December 28, 2021: Chris Altizer and Wendy Ulrich, PhD.

think about how you learned in school, in sports, at home, or at work (go ahead – think about it), you will likely agree. Similarly, opportunities for earned advantage grow with the Growth Advantage Mindset – and they don't grow with the Fixed Advantage Mindset.

Because there are so many factors that influence our mindset and because each of us is where we are at a particular point in time, there is no standard or target other than growing from where you are. However fixed or growth your mindset may be about advantage, there's an opportunity to expand it from where it is. This isn't a test you pass or fail, but a choice you make to see where you are and where you might want to be.

Working with Advantage Mindset – the framework

Mindset begins with beliefs and, as the team discovered, beliefs are influenced through exploration and choices. After working through the initial challenges of *recognizing* advantage, you can begin *working with* advantage by examining your Advantage Mindset. You can do this here in the book, in our online survey,[3] in candid discussion with others, or in combination.

Like every self-assessment, it's sometimes hard to know if we're assessing ourselves as we'd like to be or actually are. It's hard because, being human, we aren't always at our best despite our best intentions. We'll explore intentions more later, but we'll start with some of the beliefs and reactions common to advantage concepts.

---

[3] Growing the Elephant, "Growth Advantage Mindset?" Available from www.growingtheelephant.com/growth-advantage-mindset   [accessed May 5, 2022].

Fixed Advantage Mindset – FAM	Growth Advantage Mindset – GAM
1. Believes opportunities for earned advantages are finite – there are only so many.	Believes opportunities for earned advantages are abundant and can be expanded.
2. Reflects on their own experience related to advantage as all they need to know.	Reflects on their own experience related to advantage as just one part of what they need to know.
3. Believes discussions about unearned advantage are problematic and only make things worse.	Believes discussions about unearned advantage are necessary, if uncomfortable, and the only path to expanding opportunities.
4. Believes everyone has the same opportunity to earn advantage at the same level of effort.	Believes those with unearned advantages have more opportunity for earned advantage.
5. Avoids the discomfort of asking themselves "tough questions" about unearned advantage.	Will face the discomfort of tough questions to learn and grow earned advantage from unearned advantage.
6. Believes they are bad people if they have unconscious biases.	Believes everyone has unconscious biases that are only addressed by raising them.
7. Awareness: Sees themselves as they want to be experienced by others.	Awareness: Sees themselves as they actually are experienced by others.

8. Tend to aggress, avoid, freeze, or appease in response to discussions of unearned advantage.	Tend to engage, including assertively and to productively disagree, in discussions of unearned advantage.
9. Avoids seeking feedback on their own words or behavior related to advantage.	Is open to or seeks feedback from others on their words and behavior related to advantage.
10. Feels threatened by discussions of expanding opportunity for earned advantage – win/lose, net-zero for self.	Feels discussions of expanding opportunity for earned advantage lead to win/win, net-gain for all, including self.

As you explore the differences between the FAM and the GAM, you may find some aspects of the FAM to be comfortable and some of the GAM to be uncomfortable – and vice-versa. The initial assessment of Advantage Mindset is its own growth experience – and growth stretches us. We'll now explore this elephant more closely. Take your time as you read the descriptions and, for the moment, set aside explaining why you might feel one way or another.

1. Finite vs. abundant earned advantages

The FAM focuses on *constraints* of time, resources, scarcity, competition, "luck," and other factors outside of one's control that limit the opportunities for earned advantage. The GAM recognizes that opportunities *are created* by intentional action and expanded through cooperation in time and with resources within the collaborators' influence. The FAM isn't necessarily hoarding or looking to take earned advantage from others but sees through a lens of limitation rather than abundance. Seeing through a lens of abundance, the GAM recognizes that there's not only enough to go around but that, properly understood, earned advantage can be grown without limit.

2. Experiences – mine vs. others

The FAM focuses on its own experiences of advantage as the "source of truth" and is skeptical of the experiences of others where they are different. The GAM values its own experiences of advantage as the beginning of understanding the entire range of how people experience advantage and seeks to understand experiences different from its own. The FAM explains away the different negative (or positive) experiences of others as exceptions or rare cases without recognizing the protective role of unearned advantage. The GAM recognizes and works with the reality of others' negative (or positive) experiences to develop understanding and, perhaps, empathy and compassion.

3. Unearned advantage discussions – problematic vs. necessary

The FAM focuses on the inevitable discomfort that arises in recognizing and working with advantage, and fears conversations only heighten tensions and resentments. The GAM recognizes that expanding opportunities is worth the discomfort and believes discussions, even uncomfortable ones, are not only valuable but the only path forward. The FAM may recognize the need for dialogue and problem-solving, but either can't see how to work with it or can't see the tangible upsides. The GAM recognizes the need and the upsides and, as uncomfortable as it will be, sees the only way out is through.

4. Earned advantage opportunity – equal vs. unequal

The FAM holds a rule that everyone has an equal opportunity for earned advantage at the same level of effort and points out the exceptions as the rule. The GAM recognizes that while anyone can achieve earned advantage, those with unearned advantage have greater opportunities than those without them. The FAM gives little credit to tailwinds and focuses on examples of how a few without unearned advantage have overcome headwinds with great effort. The GAM recognizes the effect of tailwinds and works with the reality that the exceptions not only don't make the rule – but prove it wrong.

5. Tough questions – avoid vs. face

Similar to #3 problematic vs. necessary discussions, the FAM avoids internally exploring difficult issues of unearned advantage and avoids the "cognitive dissonance" that comes with recognizing the differences between "what is" and "how it should be." The GAM accepts that these explorations are uncomfortable but seeks to grow both its own knowledge and the opportunities for earned advantage. The FAM may fervently believe and describe equality of opportunity as right and worth fighting for – the FAM is not necessarily sexist, racist, or any other -ist. But to avoid the risk of tipping into the overwhelm zone, the FAM resists facing the reality that opportunity is not fairly distributed and will avoid exploring that part of the elephant. The GAM, perhaps due to its experience with effort, learning, and improving, can more confidently explore the growth zone without risking overwhelm.

6. Unconscious biases – "bad" people vs. "all" people

The FAM likely rejects or resists the concept of unconscious biases from an authentic sense of morality – "Being biased is bad and I'm a bad person if I am biased against different people." Unconscious biases is a particularly tough question (#5). The FAM holds that "color blind" or "gender blind" are attainable human standards as well as aspirational legal standards. Despite best intentions, while courts tell us we should strive to be blind, science and experience tells us we aren't and can't be. The GAM recognizes that all human beings carry unconscious biases that can only be managed (they can't be eliminated) when they are made conscious.

7. Sees selves – identity vs. experienced

All people typically see themselves as informed, fair, just, reasonable, funny in some fashion, and likable by those who really know them. That's human. But the FAM sees itself as it *wants to be seen* by others, its "identity" in personality terms, without insight into how it's actually experienced. The GAM sees itself *as others experience it*, typically through well-tuned awareness of self, others, and self-on-others. The GAM sees itself for what it is – for better and for worse. Facing another tough question, the FAM protects itself by focusing on intentions without awareness, "That's not what I wanted/thought/meant!" The FAM can leave a conversation mystified by how people reacted to them when others were mystified by what the FAM said or did. The GAM recognizes the differences between what it meant to convey and how people received it.

8. React/respond – stress reaction vs. intentional response

The FAM reacts to uncomfortable discussions of advantage in classic stress-induced reactions of aggression or anger (fight), avoidance (flight), inaction (freeze), or surrender (appease). The GAM responds to these discussions with developed practices of assertiveness, and even energized engagement. To be clear, no one enjoys the difficulty of these discussions and tough questions. These initial stress-induced reactions are human, inevitable, and some people – GAM or FAM – are more naturally susceptible to them than others. The GAM develops and practices skills, including the ones Maria learned in her MBSR training, to cycle through these and reduce their impact, enabling more intentional engagement with the difficult discussion.

9. Feedback – avoids vs. seeks

Because it believes it knows all it needs to know on the topic or is not equipped to face the likelihood that it doesn't know, the FAM will avoid seeking or accepting feedback from others about its behaviors or words. The GAM, because it wants to learn and knows it can improve, seeks and welcomes feedback from others as a key growth practice. The FAM may say, "I know what I know" or "That's my story and I'm sticking to it," or, more simply, "That's your problem!" The FAM may also avoid offering feedback or challenging someone because it believes it won't matter if it does. The GAM takes the position that "feedback is a gift," even if it's not easy to accept or to give. The GAM sees the potential for growth, even if only after initial rejection and upon later reflection – its own or by others.

10. Opportunity for earned advantage discussions – win/lose vs. win/win

For all the reasons we've discussed and based on #1 above, the FAM approaches discussions of expanding opportunities for earned advantage as a threat to itself: "If someone else is to gain, it must be at my expense." The GAM, on the other hand, recognizes that "rising tides float all boats" when all the boats are equally well-maintained and fitted out. Human beings are competitive by nature, some more than others. Both FAM and GAM may be fierce competitors! But because the FAM sees limited opportunities for earned advantage, and because it tends toward media messages and information sources that support its mindset, it struggles to see how others can gain without themselves having to lose. The GAM, because it sees potential to grow, and because it will test its beliefs with an intentional approach to different and diverse perspectives, sees the potential for win/win, even in a competitive world.

After reading this list, you may find yourself in either or both FAM and GAM. Take "tough questions," for example. Sometimes, you may find that you're in one or the other depending on what the questions are about! We all have moments and topics that stimulate FAM. The key Advantage Mindset question is, which are you more often and are you aware? You may find you usually have a FAM and feel conflicted about it. Or, you may find you often have a GAM and are feeling a bit smug about it.

Confused? Please, don't be.

The point of being aware of your Advantage Mindset isn't to make you feel guilty or superior.

From research and experience, we know that some people tend more naturally toward FAM, and others tend more naturally toward GAM. Mindsets have some basis in personality – so wherever you find yourself is normal and human. The question is, having FAM or GAM, can you grow from where you are?

The GAM exercise

Take a moment to settle yourself in a comfortable but alert position – perhaps sitting with feet on the floor, hands in lap, and with as erect a spine as is comfortable. Practice the breath exercise we introduced at the end of the Introduction. Give yourself a minute.

What thoughts, emotions, and sensations come up when you explore the differences between Fixed and Growth Advantage Mindsets?

Which aspects of the GAM did you find you liked or valued? Which did you find you disliked or didn't value? Which did you find yourself confused or conflicted about?

Imagine yourself having grown your Advantage Mindset from where it is today. What do you notice feeling differently for yourself? What do you notice others experiencing differently with you?

On which aspects of the GAM did you focus your attention to have grown it? Can you imagine a few of the concrete steps you took to grow it?

Now, allow yourself to release the thoughts, emotions, and sensations that arose as you considered these questions. Remember – these experiences are natural and human, just like you.

While the GAM self-assessment and reflection exercise here has been individual, the team found that talking about it helped them work with advantage and had a positive impact on their productivity and interactions. By exploring mindset, they gave themselves the permissions mentioned by Wendy Ulrich, including trying, accepting mistakes, learning from them, and improving. When their lessons learned in growing earned advantage showed up in their innovation, productivity, and collaboration, they realized how a growth mindset in one area impacts other areas.

When individuals in a group grow their collective Advantage Mindset, the positive power and impact are exponential. The larger the group, the larger the impact. To be clear – a shared growth mindset does not mean everyone agrees on a topic! In fact, a group with a Growth Advantage Mindset guarantees spirited debate and even conflict of ideas. But through these debates, improvement of organizational and societal outcomes, including diversity, equity, and inclusion outcomes, is possible. A group GAM doesn't mean "group think" – that's FAM. It does mean more people are willing to recognize and work with these difficult topics rather than ignore them.

The FAM and GAM of "lived experience"

We've used the phrase "lived experiences" a few times already, and will use it a few more. While its meaning may be obvious, by "lived experience" we mean the Oxford Reference definition of "personal knowledge about the world gained through direct, first-hand involvement in everyday events rather than through representations constructed by other people."[4] In other words,

---

[4] Oxford Reference, "Lived experience," 2022. Available from www.oxfordreference.com/view/10.1093/oi/authority.20110803100109997 [accessed May 5, 2022].

while we may accept what others tell us as truth, we know what we know from our own involvement. Believing what others tell us is a choice, a habit, or a conditioned response and we would do well to take what we hear with a grain or a shaker of salt. But believing what we ourselves have experienced is pretty obvious. In fact, it's kind of insane not to. This seems pretty simple – what could be FAM or GAM about it?

Surprisingly, a lot.

The FAM and GAM of lived experience are not about disregarding our personal knowledge gained through first-hand involvement in everyday events. What happens to us in life shapes us greatly, and is influenced by who we are and where we're from. The opportunity is to recognize that what happens to us is not necessarily what happens to others – for better and for worse.

The FAM of lived experience is, "What has happened to me happens to everyone!" Or, from another angle, "What has not happened to me does not happen to anyone!" This can cut in any direction, positive or negative. The FAM of unearned advantage considers their own lived experience as evidence that everyone, same or different, has that experience – even in the face of stronger evidence that different people do not. Research shows that people with unearned advantage have more positive interactions with people and institutions than those with less unearned advantage.[5] Those with it may be appalled by this or have trouble believing it, but it's still true. And the FAM isn't limited to those *with* unearned advantage.

---

[5] Alexandra C. Feldberg and Tami Kim, "How companies can identify racial and gender bias in their customer service." *Harvard Business Review*, May 28, 2018. Available from https://hbr.org/2018/05/how-companies-can-identify-racial-and-gender-bias-in-their-customer-service [accessed May 5, 2022].

The FAM of those with *less* unearned advantage is also limiting, but in a different way. Those with less unearned advantage have no trouble believing that companies and institutions, including government, will treat them less well given the historical facts of disparate treatment. The FAM limitation for those with less unearned advantage is expressed in extreme caution, risk aversion, and hiding or covering true feelings. There are two sides to the FAM lived experience coin:

- the FAM lived experience of those *with* unearned advantage is that things aren't bad and don't need to change (much);
- the FAM lived experience of those *with less* unearned advantage is that things aren't good but will (likely) never change.

The FAM lived experience of those with unearned advantage is that things aren't bad and don't need to change (much). The FAM lived experience of those with less unearned advantage is that things aren't good but (likely) will never change.

So, what is the GAM lived experience if "lived experience" is about what has already happened? As we said, GAM is about trying, failing, and learning. The GAM values personal knowledge through direct involvement – the trying and sometimes failing – and builds on it through learning.

The GAM recognizes that lived experiences are as varied and numerous as the individuals living them. The GAM recognizes lived experiences for what they truly represent without over-extrapolating or under-estimating their meaning. The GAM appreciates without over or under-valuing.

The GAM recognizes its lived experiences as small pieces of a much larger puzzle, and not the entire picture. In short, the GAM of lived experience is recognizing that whatever unearned advantages one does or does not have, there is an opportunity to expand earned advantage – for everyone, even if just one person at a time.

Our lived experiences shape how we engage with and respond to the world. Developing a GAM can help us recognize what is while we work toward what is possible. As we've said, developing the GAM, individual or group, isn't always easy and takes work. It requires a statement of goal and a reason why. It requires an intention.

Alvin explores intentions

Alvin, perhaps because he had less to unlearn or because he had learned so much already, struggled less with recognizing advantage than his teammates did. He wanted to "do" more about it and was working toward that end. Alvin accepted that he wasn't going to change everyone's experience with advantage, but he might influence a few people along his way. He landed on "intention setting" as a way to get started. Here's what he learned about intentions.

One dictionary definition of intention is "what one intends to do or bring about; a determination to act in a certain way."[6] That is a solid definition as far as it goes, but it's incomplete for intention-setting practice. The term "intentions" is often used interchangeably with "goals" – a statement of outcome.

An intention must include a what – a goal. That goal is a specific outcome or achievement. In addition to measurable results, it can also include holding a particular state

---

[6] Merriam-Webster, Definition of "intention," 2022. Available from www.merriam-webster.com/dictionary/intention [accessed May 5, 2022].

of mind, speaking particular words, or demonstrating deliberate actions. In Alvin's case, he wanted to grow his Advantage Mindset. Beyond a goal, however, an intention must also include a why – a purpose. The purpose drives the goal.

What (I'm doing or being) + Why (I'm doing or being it) = (My) Intention

Alvin wanted to grow his Advantage Mindset. The question for Alvin, or any of us, is "Why?" At a high level, the answer is pretty simple – to expand opportunities for earned advantage to all. That said, high-level answers to "why" questions have a way of being lost or deprioritized when things get busy or complicated. When the going gets tough, current mindsets dominate. So how can intentions help us stay the course?

Intentions – what they are, how they work

The value of setting intentions is well established. For example, in positive psychology, pioneered by author and researcher Martin Seligman, research shows that people who intentionally cultivate a positive mood are more likely to experience that positive mood.[7] That, along with other research, supports an anecdote often attributed (without proof) to the 16th U.S. President Abraham Lincoln that "Most folks are about as happy as they make up their minds to be." Lincoln's

---

[7] Brent A. Scott and Chrisopher M. Barnes, "A multilevel field investigation of emotional labor, affect, work withdrawal, and gender." *Academy of Management Journal*, 2017;54(1). https://doi.org/10.5465/amj.2011.59215086

alleged point speaks to intention – "as they make up their minds to be."

Intentions are powerful because they help us focus on what we hope to achieve without losing sight of why we want to achieve it. When intention setting becomes a practice, it's available when we need it most – the moment between what happens and our response to what happens. Psychiatrist, Holocaust survivor, and author Viktor Frankl wrote about the power of choice in his book *Man's Search for Meaning*. "The experiences of (concentration) camp life show that man does have a choice of action… Man can preserve a vestige of spiritual freedom, of independence of mind, even in such terrible conditions…"[8] A more well-known version, attributed to author Stephen Covey's writings about Frankl, is "Between stimulus and response there is a space. In that space is our power to choose our response. In our response lies our growth and our freedom."[9] Simply recognizing we have the power to choose is a power that, according to Frankl, is attainable by anyone. Our growth and freedom are reasons to choose. Choosing our response to whatever is happening is expressed and actualized through setting intentions. You grow your mindset each time you task it. It's like a muscle – work it, and it grows.

Like muscles, intentions are as flexible as they are powerful because they help us adjust our behaviors if our *What* no longer serves our *Why*. Intention setting provides both discipline and flexibility. With regular practice, you develop the ability to discern what's important and why – at the moment that such clarity is most valuable. A discipline of everyday practice makes intention setting available in high-stress situations.

---

[8] Viktor Frankl, *Man's Search for Meaning*. Beacon Press, 2006, p. 86.

[9] Alex Pattako and Elaine Dundon, *Prisoners of our Thoughts*, Berrett-Koehler Publishers, 2017, p. vi; Foreword by Stephen Covey.

Intention setting also gives us the flexibility to intentionally respond rather than habitually react to what happens around us – no matter how traumatic it may be. Frankl went on to write, "Everything can be taken… but one thing: the last of the human freedoms—to choose one's attitude in any given set of circumstances, to choose one's own way."[10] Choosing one's attitude – or mindset – is setting an intention. The ability to do this regardless of what's happening is a skill that can be improved.

Intention setting is a skill, and it improves with practice. But if we reserve it just for tough moments, it may not be available when the need arises. So instead, we intend to build intention setting into a daily habit so that it's available to us in any moment. When intention setting becomes our habitual response to what's happening, it can reduce or even replace other habitual responses we learn in life, particularly the FAM reactions of fight, flight, freeze, and appease that don't always serve us when we're *recognizing* or *working with* advantage.

Alvin decided to grow his Advantage Mindset by increasing his ability to engage in discussions of advantage without retreating or withdrawing – which was his pattern. His intention was specific, a hallmark of effective intentions, and included his "what" with his "why." "When we next talk about unearned advantages, including sexual identity, I'm going to engage and share my experience as a gay man with the team. I want to feel whole and bring my entire self to the job." Alvin decided to speak with some trusted colleagues and imagined how the conversation would unfold. He set an intention to share it in a team meeting focused on innovation and new ideas.

---

[10] Viktor Frankl, *Man's Search for Meaning*. Beacon Press, 2006, p. 87.

When he met his intention, Alvin was relieved, though not surprised, by the response from his team. What did surprise him was Maria's supportive questions and follow-up. "I don't know anyone who has come out as gay," she told him. "But I'm pretty sure I know some people who are gay but may be afraid to tell me. Do you have any advice for me?" It turned out that by growing his Advantage Mindset, Alvin created an opportunity for Maria to grow hers as well. Growth has a way of spurring growth. Intentions can support that.

Maria's GAM intention

Through her reflections and discussions, Maria felt drawn deeper into her own experiences with advantage. Having practiced the awareness of advantage reflection in Chapter 1 to recognize advantage, she decided to adapt a practice from Rhonda Magee to support *working with* advantage. You can try it out as well. It's in two parts – you can break them up or sit for the entire practice if that works for you.

Take a few moments to settle into the body in this moment and space. Feel the ground beneath you. Rest in the sensation of being in this moment.

Part 1

Breathe naturally and with ease and reflect on this question: Why am I reading this book?

Note whatever answer arises. Then, release that answer completely. Allow the feeling and thoughts, images, or stories that have come to you to fade back or away.

Breathe naturally, in and out, for several cycles of breath, settling into this moment.

Now, ask yourself: What feelings or thoughts brought me to reading *Growing the Elephant?*

Take a few minutes with this inquiry.

Allow whatever insight that might arise to be present.

Ask yourself: Where do I see unearned advantage up close?

How do unearned advantages – mine and others – touch me?

What passing thoughts, feelings, or comments of mine reflect unearned advantages?

What ideas about unearned advantages and opportunities for earned advantage did I pick up from my environment – friends, family, media?

Now, allow these thoughts, sensations, and emotions to fade back or away, to drift off into space. Let them go.

And this is, perhaps, the most essential part of the practice: see if you can be present to any discomfort, annoyance, or pain that remains. If it's intense, allow some space.

Part 2

Now come back gently to a reflection on your intentions.

What really draws you to this work? Are you seeking something you don't have or avoiding something you do have? Or are you seeking clarity? If you are seeking something, see if you can name what it is. Then, allow yourself to accept what arises without judgment.

Take a full breath, inhaling a sense of accepting what is present with as little judgment as possible. What is here, is here.

Is there a particular part of the Growth Advantage Mindset you hope to expand in yourself? Which part? How will expanding it create opportunities? Is there any sense of I'm-Fixed-and-I-can't-Grow that feels challenging?

What intentions can you set for specific parts of the GAM? Which ones will you most likely be *working with?*

Be gentle with yourself as you let these many thoughts, hopes, and plans come into focus.

If you can, take a few minutes and make notes about what you have explored and the intentions that have grown from it.

Close with a reflection on the intentions you are setting. Remember that intentions include "what" and "why."

The GAM of where you're from

You may recall that where you're from is one of the sources of unearned advantage. One example was community upbringing and Maria's faith experience in her religion. Another part of the elephant is the conflicts within and across communities regarding unearned advantages, traditions, inclusion, and even morality.

Institutions and communities of every kind struggle with and are sometimes torn by questions of who is or isn't included or what is or isn't acceptable. Having the power to decide these things is a massive source of advantage – and it's typically unearned. Religious, ethnic, and cultural traditions and norms are powerful forces that have built, sustained, and also divided and sundered communities and nations. The GAM of where you're from is not to disregard your considered beliefs or moral codes but to be open to working with differences where (and if) they (actually) exist; to bring some attention to the common humanity of where we all are from.

The GAM of where we're from recognizes that what it "knows" about "those people" is primarily informed by the story-telling of others rather than its own direct experience. We all learn from what others tell us – that's human and the foundation of parenting and any education system. Unfortunately, in this age of social media and selective perspective, it's at best incomplete and at worst heavily biased toward stereotypes. It's simpler and more convenient to not challenge stereotypes that reinforce our beliefs – it's less to think about and more comfortable than challenging what you think you know.

The news we follow is easier to listen to when told from the perspective we already hold. Who's good and who's bad, who should be allowed and who should be prevented, these ideas are simpler to keep straight when our chosen sources of authority describe other people with labels rather than as individual people. It is always more comfortable to be *fixed* than *growth* – until conditions require us to evolve or be left behind. Then it's a LOT less comfortable to remain *fixed*. And as you've undoubtedly noticed, the rate of change is increasing – and at an increasing rate.

For more perspective on growth mindset in diversity, equity, and inclusion, we highly recommend Dolly Chugh's 2018 book, *The Person You Mean to Be: How Good People Fight Bias.*

Yvonne's intention – self-compassion (and Robert's, too)

Each of our team has been trying different things working with advantage – including Yvonne. Like Robert, Yvonne found she had some FAM, though not necessarily with the same experiences or for the same reasons. But unlike Robert, she found *recognizing* advantage painfully easy. "Recognizing advantage was kind of old-hat for me," she said. "It's not hard to see what others have when you don't have it. It takes energy for me to see it and then keep on dealing with it."

From Maria, Yvonne had heard about "compassion" practices taught in different mindfulness programs. "Sounds kind of soft and fluffy," she said. Like many, Yvonne initially confused "compassion" with "empathy" or "sympathy." It's different from both. Sympathy is feeling badly for someone else's experience but not necessarily relating to it. Empathy is being able to relate to someone else's experience but not necessarily doing anything about it. Compassion is empathy *with intent to act.* Compassion for others, particularly those different from you, takes some work to develop. Robert had sympathy and empathy and was shuffling toward compassion, "What am I supposed to DO?!" he had authentically asked. Alvin's intention to bring his entire self to work was moving to an even more challenging form of compassion – self-compassion.

At Maria's recommendation, Yvonne started working with audio recordings and reading up on self-compassion from experts like Kristin Neff, Sharon Salzberg, and others. With practice over a few months, which is required to change any behavior, Yvonne realized some benefits from self-compassion. "Turns out compassion provides the energy I need to face and deal with what's happening," she said.

Like Yvonne, you might initially find the whole idea "soft and fluffy"! If so, do you recall in *recognizing* advantage how we said a child could more easily than an adult see the entire elephant? When you were a child, or even now, you likely found both comfort and recovery in "soft and fluffy." The practice described here is adapted from the work of these experts and is highly recommended.

Go ahead, get soft and fluffy. No one is here to judge you.

Advantage compassion – for Yvonne and Robert (and the rest of us)

As you have with other exercises, come to a comfortable posture, noticing points of contact with the floor and chair and sensations of air and temperature on the body. Notice your breathing – perhaps beginning with a full breath in and out, then allowing its natural pattern.

Bring to mind any memories of your experience with unearned advantage – your own or that of others.

Notice what thoughts or feelings are arising? Sadness, guilt, resentment, pain? It can be difficult to name feelings more specifically than "bad" or "unpleasant" – that's true for all of us. See if you can "stand back" from the feelings and describe them as if you were observing them. If this gets too difficult, you can "stand back" and notice something else nearby that's neutral or supportive. Be kind – this is hard work.

Notice any sensations in the body, focusing on where they are most felt in this moment.

Breathe in and sense more deeply into these feelings. Notice where they might be felt in the body – shoulders, neck, belly, head, chest? What sensations accompany them? Similar to noticing thoughts and feelings, if noticing sensations becomes too challenging, step back mentally (or even physically) for the space you need to remain. Earlier, we said sometimes you need to STOP to be able to go. That works here, too.

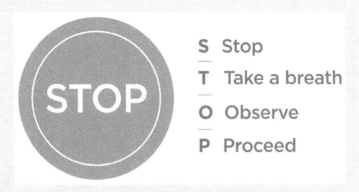

S   Stop

T   Take a breath

O   Observe

P   Proceed

Image credit: Maria Laura Garza

As you can *proceed*, breathe naturally but fully as you allow more and more awareness of these thoughts, feelings, and sensations.

Now, begin to sense into your compassion for yourself in this moment. Allow yourself to be willing to be free from the discomfort and pain of what is present. See what choices you can make about what thoughts and feelings you intentionally cultivate, allow, or release. If it feels right, consider placing one hand over your heart and another over your belly. Or one hand on your forehead and another toward the back of your neck.

As you do, notice the sense of support you can grow from your own compassionate contact with each breath.

Now, call to mind a person or living creature who has been a loving support to you in your life. If none come to mind, consider a person from history who has inspired you in your life. Several may come to mind – pick one image that resonates strongly in this moment for this visualization practice.

Visualization comes easier to some than others – just like *working with advantage.* However it is for you in this moment, breathe in and out with openness, making the image as vivid as you can. Notice sensations of support, solidarity, kindness, or love that arise with this image.

Allow any thoughts or feelings of struggle or judgment that arise for you to simply fade back or away. Settle into your natural breath, breathing in compassion and breathing out struggle or judgment.

Continue to hold the image in mind for two to three minutes – you can even set a timer if you like. As your mind wanders, return it to this vivid image of support and growth. Sense into your feelings and thoughts – what sources of strength, resilience, insight, compassion, or other positives are there that you haven't noticed recently?

Now, see if you can imagine expanding these positives beyond your physical body. Imagine expanding them to some people who you care for, wherever they may be. Bask in the sensation of growing these positives.

If you are willing, imagine expanding these positives to others like you struggling with *recognizing* or *working with* unearned advantage. If that can happen, imagine expanding these positives to others, unlike you, who are struggling with it. Finally, imagine expanding these positives to anyone struggling with any experiences of pain or suffering.

When you are ready, allow the many images that have come to mind and been held to drift away. Then, begin returning your attention to yourself. Take a few minutes to remain in this awareness – simply sitting and breathing.

This practice promotes motive and energy to grow compassion – empathy with intent to act. Compassion, for self and for others, helped Robert put a dent into the guilt and resentment cycle that had kept him from developing intentions as Maria and Alvin had. It also helped Yvonne release some of the frustration and resentment that had held her in place without disowning or denying it. As "soft and fluffy" as it sounds, compassion practice can be a powerful tool in *recognizing* and *working with* unearned advantage and growing earned advantage. Surprisingly enough, practicing compassion supports a key attribute required for growing earned advantage – courage.

As you probably experienced in the previous chapter, recognizing unearned advantage requires courage to see the entire elephant. Whether you hold a lot or a little, working with advantage isn't easy. In this chapter, you have probably experienced how working with unearned advantage also requires courage – to come into contact with the different and scary parts of it without fighting, flighting, freezing, or appeasing. In the next chapter, we'll see how growing earned advantage also requires courage – to harness or even climb onto the elephant to steer it toward growing earned advantage for all.

Chapter summary

In this chapter, you've focused on *working with* advantage, the elephant in the room. That takes courage! You've identified and developed some valuable muscles, including Growth Advantage Mindset (GAM), intention setting, and compassion.

By *working with* unearned advantage, whether you have a little or a lot, you can courageously develop the skills and resilience needed to grow your mindset and capacity to *grow* earned advantage.

Working with advantage – reflection

As you have read about our team and their stories, what resonated with you in your experience?

Which of the practices in this chapter came more easily to you? Did any come with difficulty? Were any beyond what you wanted or felt you could do? Consider rereading or replaying these at different times and settings. If you're comfortable working with them, consider discussing your experiences with trusted others.

Another helpful practice you can explore is journaling. Consider repeating any of these practices and jotting down your thoughts and responses. You might even let that become its own practice as you continue to explore this elephant.

Chapter 3: Growing earned advantage

Unconscious biases – seriously uncomfortable...

“THAT was even MORE irritating than that seminar!” Robert had just taken an Implicit Association Test (IAT). “It turns out I’m biased against EVERYONE ELSE!!” The Harvard IAT (see Resources) measures the strength of associations between concepts (e.g., skin color, sexual identity, etc.) and evaluations (e.g., good, bad) or stereotypes (e.g., athletic, clumsy). It’s free to take – sort of. It stresses the heart and pushes the mind. In short, it gives you feedback about what implicit associations, or unconscious biases, you hold. There are several different IATs, each challenging in its way.

Robert’s experience is typical of people like him. It is also typical of people different from him. In fact, it is typical of all human beings. The uncomfortable truth about unconscious biases is that we all hold them because they are a deeply wired survival trait. We touched on this earlier in *recognizing* advantage and now get a bit deeper. Growing earned advantage involves deeply understanding our individual reactions to sources of unearned advantage of who you are and where you’re from.

From our earliest origins, humans looked for indicators that an approaching human was similar or different in appearance in order to stay alive and thrive. While it's nice to think we've all grown beyond that, recall your earlier exercise in the meeting/cafeteria (p. 30)? If you're skeptical, the research is as abundant as it is uncomfortable – as Robert found out.

Robert took the IAT a few times. He also looked for evidence that the whole idea wasn't all it was purported to be. He couldn't help a thought that jumped to mind: "Maybe liberal Harvard just *wants* me to feel like a racist?" Now, it was Robert's turn to feel as conflicted as Maria had done. He had been recognizing and working with advantage, but growing it had begun to feel like he, and others with unearned advantages, were being led toward giving up earned advantages in a zero-sum game of winners and losers. He began to associate the entire process with even more challenging topics of who can be "married," the teaching of "Critical Race Theory," and other intense debates about government policies and social movements associated with advantage. At times, it became overwhelming, and he just wanted to quit thinking about it. Sometimes, the elephant just seems too big.

This thought-chain, and others like it, comes as naturally as unconscious biases – they are all basic survival instincts. And because they are about survival, we feel them more strongly than just about anything. Because we're human, we'll do whatever's required to stay alive. But at the same time, because we're human, we can also form and expand community beyond our most basic similarities to not only survive but to thrive. Robert was surprised to learn that Yvonne had a similar reaction taking the Weight IAT, Maria the Skin-Tone IAT, and Alvin the Disability IAT. "OK," he said, "It's not just me!" Then, with some reflection, he added, "And I'm not a racist, right?"

Like Robert and most people, Maria also found she had unconscious biases. In her case, one was toward sexual orientation. Her earlier conversations with Alvin had helped her realize that unconscious biases are, first and foremost – unconscious. After talking with Alvin, she was more aware of her biases. Being aware of her biases, in a positive irony, helped her avoid working from underlying assumptions about LGBTQ people. Once conscious of her biases, her awareness informed both her perceptions and her behaviors. While she struggled to accept that she – and every person – has unconscious biases, she realized that she could minimize their influence through awareness.

Little things that add up

As each experimented with the IAT, they understood that *having* biases didn't necessarily mean they *acted* with biases. As each realized, having biases is human – everyone has them. They also realized that ignoring or pretending they didn't is naïve and has a darker side. Choosing to ignore the reality of biases makes it easier for those who do choose to cultivate or exploit them. Choosing to *cultivate or exploit* biases crosses into racist, sexist, or any other -ist that supports unearned advantage and reduces the equal opportunity for earned advantage. There are, unfortunately, and dangerously, people in the world who believe in and work toward taking advantage based on who you are or where you're from. Those are cultivated, even curated, conscious biases – big things that fill human history and, sadly, today's news. Recognizing that, we're pretty sure that those people are not reading *Growing the Elephant*. Those reading this book have more in common with our team members, including Alvin.

"I don't think anyone on this project would consciously discriminate," Alvin said. "No one would tolerate that." Then, he reflected for a moment, "But even the 'little things' add up – even if I think no one means it."

When learning about intentions, Alvin had learned how setting intentions gave some protections against "I wish I hadn't said that" and "That's not what I meant." He had realized that so much of what we say in casual conversation is from habit rather than intent – but still has an impact. Alvin himself used the phrase, "That's so GAY!" to make fun of something. Maria often referred to "the girls" in the office, and others also used phrases or words, even if just between their friends, that had the power to offend or even stun others, if used differently.

One of the many tensions in *growing* advantage is recognizing that language and its ownership is powerful and cultural. Language springs from where you're from, a source of unearned advantage *and* a source of identity, pride, and motivation.

The turbulence of language ownership – claiming the baggage

(Warning – potentially offending words inbound!)

When flying – and when recognizing sources of advantage – you are flying with or against tailwinds and headwinds. When working with advantage, you're going to hit rough spots or turbulence. The "ownership of language" we mentioned is one of those rough spots we all fly through. Earlier, Alvin described something as "so gay," and Maria said "the girls." More intense examples are phrases like "Resting Bi*#@ Face" referring to women and the more than a few terms we won't print here referring to women, LGBTQ, Hispanics, Black people, Asians, people with disabilities, and pretty much every minority community. Some members of these communities use these words between or about themselves, and some don't. However, what is clear is that when non-members of the communities use these words, the impact is significant and negative. Why is that?

The issue is directly related to unearned advantage. As long as there have been differences between people resulting in power imbalances, language has been a cultural support to those imbalances. For centuries to the current day, these offensive terms, the baggage of unearned advantage, have been used by some of those *with* unearned advantages to describe, differentiate, and deny those *without* them. When those holding unearned advantages use any of these terms, it still has that offensive effect. Fewer than in the past? Yes. Still a thing? Obviously. So, why do some people without unearned advantages use these terms? Why would someone with dark skin use "the N-word" or a woman use "the B-word" or any of the other examples? Why do they claim this baggage?

For many people with less unearned advantage, claiming the baggage is exerting ownership. These derogatory terms have long been used as weapons by individuals and systems supporting unearned advantage. When those without advantages claim them, there is a sense that the weapons can no longer be turned on them. Are there derogatory terms for those with unearned advantage, particularly White or male? Yes – a few. Have those terms been historically, currently, *and effectively* weaponized against them? Not at all.

There is, however, an opportunity for greater awareness of the entire elephant when it comes to language ownership. We'll start with the obvious – those holding unearned advantages should be aware that claiming that baggage, using those words, is an overt aggression and intentional insult

– a macro-aggression. By definition, it can't be funny and it's never a "little thing."

On the other hand, those without unearned advantages may claim a right to the baggage. They carried it for others for centuries – it's theirs to own. That said, they can also be aware of how claiming it may disturb people similar to them who would prefer it be left to history. Language can be either habitual or intentional and impact similar people differently.

And by claiming that baggage, those without unearned advantages can confuse those people *with* unearned advantage who don't use and condemn its use by others like them. "I would NEVER use that word to describe a Black person – I don't know why my Black friends do," Alvin said. Alvin, and other folks like him, rarely commit those macro-aggressions. They are more likely, however, to trip into "micro-aggressions."

"Little things" – micro-aggressions

Micro-aggressions are behaviors or words used by those with unearned advantages that (unintentionally) highlight or reinforce those unearned advantages. "Micro" is a crucial modifier – these are "little things" that those with unearned advantages *don't recognize* as references to who you are or where you're from. Yet, the very idea of micro-aggressions generates as much heat in DEI programs as the concept of "privilege," as these examples show.

Maria is constantly being asked to set up lunch by one male colleague, Carl, reflecting his unconscious bias about the role of women as caregivers or even servers. "But I didn't mean that," Carl said when challenged. "I respect women for professional competence, and I advocate for them in talent reviews! I wish she'd told me how she felt!" Maria thought about that. "Why is it on me to tell him what he should already know? It's easier just to say, 'I can't do that right now,' than make a big deal and explain how it makes me feel."

Yvonne, with her background and education, is often complimented for being "articulate" when presenting or expressing her ideas. "It's not that I mind the compliment, but I do mind the tone of surprise as they say it." That Yvonne takes any offense at being complimented stunned Alex, one executive. "You mean I can't say she did a good job? My tone? My look? I don't understand. What AM I supposed to say? I guess I'll just say NOTHING from now on and be safe!"

We'll explore this notion of "safe" for those with unearned advantage later. But for now, and for *growing*, let's increase awareness of what each of these characters is experiencing as they experience it.

Awareness of micro-aggression

Before putting yourself into these different experiences, take a few minutes to get centered. Then, as you have with other exercises, come to a comfortable posture, noticing points of contact with the floor and chair and sensations of air and temperature on the body. Next, notice your breathing – perhaps beginning with a full breath in and out, and then allowing its natural pattern.

Begin by bringing Carl to mind. Imagine he's your colleague where you work or volunteer – someone you know, typically respect, and generally like. Or imagine you are Carl. Reflect on the moment he recognizes his habit of who he asks to deal with lunch and its impact on them. Reflect on his anger

– and embarrassment – at being challenged to act differently. How might he apply STOP to his reaction? What are simple intentions he could set to grow earned advantage with his newfound awareness?

When done, allow your thoughts and feelings about Carl to fade and reconnect to the sensations of sitting where you are. If this exercise was challenging, consider it a success and pick this up another time. Otherwise, you might proceed.

Bring Maria to mind. Imagine she's your colleague – or you. Reflect on her sense of annoyance and resignation at Carl's repeated behavior. What responses can you choose for her to Carl's question, "Why didn't you tell me?" Imagine that dialogue and how she could assertively "call-in" Carl to communicate her experience and what she could ask of him. Imagine how Carl would likely respond. What simple intention can she set for responding to this situation in the future?

When done, allow your thoughts and feelings about Maria to fade and reconnect to the sensations of sitting where you are. If this exercise was challenging, consider it a success and pick this up another time. Otherwise, you might proceed.

Bring Alex to mind. Imagine he's your colleague – or you. Reflect on his belief that complimenting performance unaided by unearned advantages *should be* received as a compliment. Reflect on the moment he recognizes that how he delivers compliments to others can be received as a reminder of unearned advantages. Reflect on his indignation at being challenged to act differently and confusion about how to do that. How might he apply STOP to his reaction? What are simple intentions he could set to grow earned advantage with his newfound awareness?

When done, allow your thoughts and feelings about Alex to fade and reconnect to the sensations of sitting where you are. If this exercise was challenging, consider it a success and pick this up another time. Otherwise, you might proceed.

Bring Yvonne to mind. Imagine she is your colleague – or you. Reflect on her sense of annoyance and exhaustion at compliments from those with unearned advantage that highlight it. Reflect on how the repetition of this experience can impact how she can receive *any* praise. How might she apply STOP if she notices an automatically negative interpretation of what's being said? Imagine calling in Alex, responding to his confusion about what to do or avoid. What intention can Yvonne set to assertively communicate appreciation for compliments that reflect her performance without relativity to who she is or where she is from?

When you are ready, allow the many images that have come to mind and been held to drift away. Then, begin returning your attention to yourself. Take a few minutes to remain in this awareness – simply sitting and breathing.

This practice promotes motive and energy to grow earned advantage by engaging others with compassion. Compassion for others includes increasing their awareness of the impact they have when you practice "calling them in" for dialogue rather than "calling them out" to others. "Soft and fluffy" compassion turns out to be a key to getting to the "hard and edgy" of different parts of the elephant.

A little big thing – earning the benefit of the doubt

A small, but powerful, source of advantage invisible to those with more unearned advantage but obvious to those with less is getting "the benefit of the doubt." The benefit of the doubt is simply the willingness of someone to trust without verifying, believe without proof, or simply to take the risk of giving a chance despite an unproven track record. A person's willingness to place trust in or take a risk on another person is influenced by many factors, including shared traits of who you are and where you're from. Perceptions of differences based on personal experience or, and powerfully, cultural images and stereotypes are all at work. Our individual and collective experiences, including our perceptions and beliefs, conscious and unconscious, accurate and uninformed, influence our notions of who is and isn't trustworthy or deserving of the benefit of the doubt. How does this matter?

When Robert is thinking about to whom he might delegate an important task, does his perception of Yvonne's background create doubt about her ability to deliver? When Maria is thinking about inviting Alvin to speak at a meeting, is she wondering, even subconsciously, if his openness about being gay will reduce his impact – and the perception of her for picking him? Whether or not Robert or Maria are conscious of this inner dialogue – especially if they are not – it's almost certain to be present.

"Those people can't be trusted!" is not a belief held just by those with unearned advantages. Yvonne's experience of being discounted may give rise to withholding the benefit of the doubt, as well. "I wonder if Robert is giving me a break because he thinks I deserve it or he's just trying to look good?" Even if she doesn't consciously realize this thought, it could be there. Like holding unconscious biases, the benefit of the doubt is something we give without realizing the influence of differences. But the willingness to give the benefit of the doubt isn't limited to similar people. Robert may be as skeptical of another White person's track record as Yvonne is – for example, about that White person's track record on commitment or work performance. On the other hand, Yvonne may be as skeptical about another African-American's track record on commitment or work performance as Robert is. These skepticisms may come from very different perspectives, but the impact is the same. Each of us develops perceptions and beliefs about others, including those similar to ourselves. How to deal with it?

Earning the benefit of the doubt – reflection

Take a moment to settle yourself in a comfortable but alert position – as you may have practiced earlier. Practice the breath exercise we introduced at the end of the Introduction. Give yourself a minute.

Reflect on situations in your past where you have given someone "the benefit of the doubt." Bring to mind actual events, making a mental note of the different people who received this benefit from you.

Consider what factors influenced you in those situations to give the benefit of the doubt. Consider your past experiences with them or people like them. Consider your hopes or expectations of their success. Consider what traits of who you are or where you're from you have in common with them. Make mental notes of what you find.

Take a moment and allow these situations, people, and what you found to fade.

If available, reflect on situations in your past where you withheld the benefit of the doubt or allowed your skepticism to influence your decisions for a specific person. Realize that in those situations where we withheld the benefit of the doubt, our recall is often that we simply acted with prudence or to "getting things done fast" or to "not putting someone in a position to fail." Think deeply and as objectively as you can.

Consider what factors influenced you in those situations to withhold the benefit of the doubt. Consider your past experiences with them or people like them. Consider your fears or expectations of their failure. Consider what traits of who you are or where you're from you have in common. Make mental notes of what you find.

Take a moment and allow these situations, people, and what you found to fade.

It may be that you found no differences in giving or with-holding the benefit of the doubt in who you are or where you're from. It may also be that, similar to the Chapter 1 reflection of entering the cafe and deciding where to sit, you are only aware of these differences when you take the time to reflect. Similar to other reflections, what do you make of what you found? How might it inform you when considering giving the benefit of the doubt?

The benefit of the doubt is a powerful source of advantage because it provides encouragement to the untested and second chances to the still committed. Our life experiences and even our personality have much to do with our tendency to trust others. That said, when we automatically grant it to some, require earned proof from others, and sometimes withhold it altogether from others, it's worthwhile to see if who you are or where you're from is playing a role.

Claiming more baggage – unpacking gender personal pronouns

Maria and Yvonne were talking about something they had noticed during some of the virtual meetings they had been attending. "I don't understand why some people are putting 'He/Him' or 'She/Her' after their names?" Yvonne said. "I hear you," Maria replied. "Yesterday there was a new person, Chris, he – I think he's a man? He had 'They/Them' after his name. I didn't know how to refer to him? I want to respect him, but I'm not sure how?" Yvonne replied, "I saw that! I'm glad to call him – or they – whatever they want. I did an inter-net search during the call – it's like a new language! I noticed that Alvin had his pronouns listed – He/Him. But he told us he's gay? I don't get it!"

Like all aspects of every living language, personal pronouns are steeped in history, tradition, and culture. They have evolved over centuries across different languages – including English. This particular evolution of grammar, of gender personal pronouns, is no different. Yet, a casual news search will highlight the tensions arising from individuals asking that they be referred to by the pronouns they choose. In some cases, coworkers, teachers, or others refuse to meet that ask, explaining it creates awkwardness or is too much effort. Some would rather lose their jobs than use pronouns for others that *they* don't choose, citing their beliefs or religious convictions. Meanwhile, those choosing their pronouns may feel disrespected when their choices aren't honored – with or without intent. How do we unpack this baggage without spilling it all over the place?

The use of gender personal pronouns is another part of the elephant. It stems from the competing human interests to belong and, at the same time, be unique. Belonging helps us survive, while uniqueness helps us thrive. We want both, and tradition, culture, and even personality all play a role in which we value more. Some feel uniqueness is respected by choosing pronouns, while others feel belonging is threatened by being asked to respect different choices. Many are open to either but aren't sure how best to achieve both.

For example, Yvonne may not understand why Alvin, a gay man, chooses He/Him yet she may be fine with whatever pronoun he chooses. Maria may want to understand and will ask to learn. Robert may find it awkward to refer to an individual as "they" and might be annoyed with the attention he has to pay to "get it right." Alvin may also find it awkward, but is less annoyed. The more unearned advantage you have, the harder it can be to recognize the uniqueness of who you are or where you're from when the "you" is someone else. Remember – we tend not to notice the headwinds others face. We also may find it annoying when asked to help deal with baggage by sharing some of the load. Personal reflection can help us unpack the baggage.

Unpack some baggage

Take a moment to settle yourself in a comfortable but alert position – as you may have practiced earlier. Practice the breath exercise we introduced at the end of the Introduction. Give yourself a minute.

What thoughts, emotions, and sensations come up when you are asked to turn toward the topic of personal pronouns?

What is your lived experience with people who ask for non-traditional pronouns? What is your lived experience with those who seem uncomfortable using them? What do you know from your own experience versus what you have read or heard about?

What needs or concerns *of yours* are met or not met by asking for or agreeing to use non-traditional pronouns?

What needs or concerns *of others* are met or not met by asking for or agreeing to use non-traditional pronouns?

What intentions can you set regarding your use of personal pronouns?

Now, allow yourself to release the thoughts, emotions, and sensations that arose as you considered these questions. Allow that these experiences are natural and human – just like you.

Literally harder to carry – disability

These sections on language ownership and the impact of micro-aggression have focused on how people use and claim the baggage of words and descriptions of themselves and others. Who you are and where you're from include all the traits and experiences that make you the person you are today, including place of origin, race, color, religion, gender, sexual identity, and age.

Disability – as in having or not having a physical or cognitive disability – is another aspect of who you are. According to the World Health Organization, in 2020, over one billion people on the planet lived with a disability.[1] As of 2018, in the

---

[1] World Health Organization, "Disability and health fact sheet," November 24, 2021. Available from www.who.int/news-room/fact-sheets/detail/disability-and-health [accessed March 11, 2022].

U.S. one in four adults lived with a disability.[2] These are huge numbers that are close to home – but are not easy to see.

For example, as a parent of a child with a learning disability, Robert has navigated how to talk about "people with disabilities" rather than "disabled people." He has learned, and is still learning, that neutral language can feel right to people without disabilities but is condescending to people with disabilities. Robert has the unearned advantage of not needing to face the headwind of having a disability – he just has to support his son as his son flies into that headwind. Other members of the team will likely face this challenge themselves or with loved ones in the form of physical, emotional, mental, or addiction challenges. Being born with or developing a disability – or not – is part of who you are. Members of the team will almost certainly face this challenge with people they don't necessarily know. They may not even be aware if the challenge is present.

Yvonne found herself becoming annoyed by a new requirement at work to add close captioning to videos and alternative text to image files. "To my knowledge, we don't serve any hearing or visually-impaired people with these products," she said. It only took a moment's reflection, however, for her to realize the irony of that statement. She also realized the power of this commitment not only to those who benefit from these enhancements but to the broader understanding of accessibility, regardless of ability.

The range of disabilities, physical, intellectual, neurological, and mental, is wide and can be present from birth, through development, and through accident or injury. Millions of

---

[2] Catherine A. Okoro, NaTasha D. Hollis, Alissa C. Cyrus, and Shannon Griffin-Blake, "Prevalence of disabilities and health care access by disability status and type among adults — United States, 2016." *Morbidity and Mortality Weekly Report* (MMWR), 2018;67: 882–887. http://dx.doi.org/10.15585/mmwr.mm6732a3

U.S. servicemen and women have one or more disabilities connected with military service.[3] The impact of disability is not only felt in the quality of life of those with disabilities and their caregivers but in how the world interacts with them. Mental health challenges figure prominently in reported high-stakes interactions with law enforcement, particularly for those with fewer unearned advantages.[4] Robert's son faces the headwind of disability, but fewer headwinds than, say, someone with the same disability but of color or an immigrant.

Not having a disability is simply another unearned advantage that can't be given back or away. That said, whatever unearned advantages we're talking about of who you are or where you're from, whether you hold many or few, there is an opportunity to grow earned advantage. There is an opportunity to extend compassion and grow the good.

Grow the good – feel the real

In his work, psychologist and author Rick Hanson, Ph.D., teaches about well-being and psychological growth. He talks about how you can "grow the good that lasts" through simple practices that allow experiences to become learning and learning to become lasting change. These are particularly helpful when the experiences you're having are challenging or transforming how you've thought, felt, or acted in your life. We're adapting his work here and highly recommend

---

[3] Statista Research Department, "U.S. veterans by disability status 2019," January 27, 2022. Available from www.statista.com/statistics/250316/us-veterans-by-disability-status/ [accessed March 11, 2022].

[4] Abigail Abrams, "Black, disabled and at risk: The overlooked problem of police violence against Americans with disability." *Time Magazine*, June 25, 2020. Available from https://time.com/5857438/police-violence-black-disabled/ [accessed May 5, 2022].

him for further reading on topics of resilience, calm, and confidence. We'll start with Robert.

When the case of George Floyd, an American Black man suffocated to death in public by a White policeman in the U.S., came to national prominence in 2020, Robert had a revelation. "I realized a cop would never execute me for passing a counterfeit $20 bill – because of Who I Am." While he was aware of the history of Black people in America, this event reached him in a profoundly different way. He had not reconciled the past with the present until this particular event gave him no choice.

However, while that was Robert's experience, many other people had the same initial experience but processed it differently. Some developed various reasons for why George Floyd was killed or that he wasn't murdered at all. Even as the policeman was convicted of murder, some felt the trial was unfair or politically influenced. Why is that?

These are the scariest parts of the elephant. The current reality that Black people in America and other nations, or Asians in the age of COVID, or Hispanics or others seeking asylum from war or famine, or LGBTQ who are simply using a restroom, are treated unjustly and even fatally *because of who they are* is too disturbing or difficult for some to accept. Even those holding only a few unearned advantages, or perhaps because of that, deny these realities. The Fixed Advantage Mindset can accept any single example of discrimination due to unearned advantage as an exception – but it often cannot accept a pattern of them as a rule.

The Fixed Advantage Mindset can accept any single example of discrimination due to unearned advantage as an exception – but it often cannot accept a pattern of them as a rule.

Exploring this part of the elephant is the hardest to do. So, how did Robert process it differently?

Robert felt the need to integrate this experience into his reality. So, he applied a lesson from Hanson's work, described here in three steps:

- Be with the experience.
- Turn the experience into a feeling.
- Focus on what you can learn from it.

Robert's application of the process went like this:

1. First, he recognized this difficult experience and used practices from this book to be with it. "It's ironic – I know – that *I* should have trouble thinking about what happened to George Floyd or the other recent cases of injustice." Second, Robert reflected on the realization that he was safe from so many forms of violence – including from authority. Third, he worked through conflicting feelings of anger for this injustice, a seemingly irresolvable sense of guilt for not "doing something," and the unavoidable desire to simply stop thinking about it. By staying with it, Robert began converting his experience into his learning.

2. Over some time, in his case a few days, but some may find over months (or a lifetime), Robert focused on recognizing and describing his negative feelings so he could let them go. He began working with "what is" rather than "what should be" and accepted the realities and threats of injustice faced by others without unearned advantages. Through this, he began to think that maybe he could "do something," to expand opportunities for earned advantage. Robert started to convert his learning into change.

3. Robert sought to grow earned advantage within his scope of influence – which was broader than he first thought. He realized that he could support others, including but not just Yvonne, simply by acknowledging what was happening in the world. Robert's willingness to engage in these most challenging issues was the Growth Advantage Mindset in action.

Robert had converted his experience into lasting change. In other words, he was planting the seeds of earned advantage. He wasn't the only member of the team digging into this soil.

The events and coverage surrounding the murder of George Floyd impacted Yvonne as well. Her grow the good, feel the real experience, which extended beyond herself, went like this:

1. Yvonne had to address how she thought, felt, and acted. Her experience witnessing the murder of George Floyd and the reaction of many people with unearned advantage threw her into deep trauma on many levels. At first, she was confused that her anger about their reactions seemed to eclipse her sense of horror from seeing the video footage over and over again. She avoided conversations with anyone who was not a person of color and resorted to sleep whenever she started to imagine things she'd say to them. She woke from weird, unclear nightmares. She could not concentrate or eat for days.

2. Yvonne realized she could not "be with the experience" because her feelings were overwhelming, so she sought counseling through her church. Through talk therapy, the counselor helped her process her experiences reacting to the death of George Floyd and she discovered she was being retraumatized. As a young

teenager, Yvonne complained to her mother and uncle about multiple sexual advances from a 30-year-old man who was a friend of the extended family. Her mother and adults in her life denied that there were so many advances, saying "men will be men" and her uncle blamed her for "acting fresh" when they saw first hand how the family friend grabbed her buttocks with both hands during an embrace at a family picnic exclaiming, "Girl, you sure are growing up healthy!" The counselor helped her realize that she and George Floyd had more in common than she had imagined. Both of them were disbelieved, blamed wrongly, and were victims of injustices that are disproportionately experienced in the United States by human beings just because they are Black. Research and interventions about this bias called "adultification" are an increasing focus. People of goodwill are exploring how to eliminate mistreatment of Black girls who are not getting the benefits of being viewed as innocent – by law enforcement, people in the legal system, and by family and community members.[5]

3. Yvonne sought to share her learnings with others committed to growing advantage. While she chose not to share the details of her challenging personal experiences with "adultification," she did make a point in the DEI learning sessions to describe how trauma manifests and why. She talked about the power of individuals to move beyond trauma, and about improvements

---

[5] Georgetown Law News, "Research confirms that Black girls feel the sting of adultification bias identified in earlier Georgetown Law study," May 15, 2019. Available from www.law.georgetown.edu/news/research-confirms-that-black-girls-feel-the-sting-of-adultification-bias-identified-in-earlier-georgetown-law-study/ [accessed May 5, 2022].

in her leadership as a university administrator. As a direct result of her deeper understanding of the potential effects of trauma, Yvonne encouraged leaders within her sphere of influence to learn about this issue and consider providing information and resources to support faculty, staff, and students.

Yvonne found Maria to be particularly pensive in the discussion. In the session, Maria realized that she sometimes dismissed stories about discrimination told by brown-skinned-immigrants at her church, saying to herself – and sometimes to those people out loud – "All immigrants and people with accents are mistreated the same everywhere in this country! Why is anyone complaining?" It occurred to her that their lived experiences were different from hers precisely because most people perceive she is White, and that perception confers some difference in treatment compared to people of color, her accent notwithstanding. "I might have learned more from them if I listened more to them," she said to Alvin, as she shook her head.

Alvin, on the other hand, was hearing things from Yvonne that confirmed behaviors he already knew but hadn't quite noticed in himself. "Wow, this conversation really is making me think about things. I mean, I am now thinking how I know for a fact that I routinely assume anybody older than 50 who complains about not being given a fair chance at the company is totally exaggerating. Heck, I have even blamed a few of them for not trying hard enough in our fast-paced tech world without hearing them out. That's insane. And I definitely need to think twice about whether we're set up to listen for what's going on and not just to the people complaining."

Each of our team, in their own way and yet together, are finding ways to grow the good and feel the real. Recognizing an uncomfortable reality, particularly when it conflicts with how we believe the world should be, is hard. Working with that reality, particularly when it challenges us to reconsider our role in that world, as small or as large as it is, is also hard. But as hard as these things are, we can grow the good when we reflect on our experiences, get support when we need it, and engage others along the way. Each member of our team is planting seeds of earned advantage. And like all seeds, these seeds need watering.

Watering the seeds of earned advantage – RAIN

R Recognize

A Accept

I Investigate

N Natural Awareness

Image credit: Maria Laura Garza

Between Grow the Good, Growing the Elephant, Growth Zone, and Growth Advantage Mindset, you may feel an inevitable cultivation analogy coming on – and here it is. A valuable framework in growing earned advantage is RAIN – Recognize, Accept, Investigate, and Natural Awareness (also called Non-Identification). Initially created by mindfulness teacher Michele McDonald and shared by experts including Diana Winston, Tara Brach, and others, RAIN has many uses – including Growing the Elephant by *growing* earned advantage.

R – Recognize. You've been practicing *recognizing* advantage already, along with some skills that help you see what's there to be seen, rather than what you'd like to see or think should be seen. When you *recognize*, you can see below the surface and through the clouds to sources of both earned and unearned advantage. Celebrate your ability to *recognize*.

A – Accept. Through some of the practices you've experimented with, you've been working on *accepting* what is there to be seen and felt with less emotional or judgmental reaction to unearned advantage. When you *accept*, you acknowledge what is real, regardless of how you feel about it. **Key point** – you *accept* that something is what it is *in this moment*. Accept *does not* mean you intend to allow it to go unchallenged or unchanged. If Accept feels like too much of a stretch, try using Allow and see if that feels more possible. Accepting, or even *allowing*, that something is present can be very challenging!

I – Investigate. Through working with and growing, you've been *investigating* your own relationships to sources of advantage. Investigate involves asking yourself "tough" questions and remaining steady as you find uncomfortable answers. Several of the exercises you've completed already were *investigations*. When you *investigate*, you explore your entire reaction to what is happening – how you feel in body and mind and spirit. When you *investigate*, you may need to STOP if what you're finding is too intense or if you come out of your "window of tolerance." Investigate is not a competition or a race – pace yourself.

N – Natural Awareness. Also known as Non-identification or Nurturing, Natural Awareness is the ability to separate what you've seen, felt, or thought from who you are. For example, in the Fixed Advantage Mindset, recognizing unconscious biases stimulates, "I'm a BAD person!" In the Growth Advantage Mindset, you understand unconscious biases to be natural to all of us. Natural Awareness, a GAM enabler, is the ability to not be attached to a single point of view or a limited experience as "the truth." Natural Awareness allows you to see yourself and others as *more* than a label or set of demographic traits *without losing the relevance of those traits.* Natural Awareness helps us realize that "color blind" is not natural or helpful. It provides that you *do* see and experience color, age, gender, ability – and any differences – as respecting those differences. It also allows you to make conscious what is typically unconscious so you can make intentional choices about what thoughts you cultivate, words you speak, and things you do.

The RAIN framework is a key foundation of *Growing the Elephant.* It's not quite RAINing earned advantage yet, but all the clouds are here, and the breeze is right. You've heard some thunder and seen some lightning. Many of the practices you've experienced so far in the book may have been new or novel. Some good news! Several management practices have been around that also contribute to growing earned advantage. We explore them in a bit – after we claim one more bit of language baggage.

Claiming "woke" – RAIN and the Growth Advantage Mindset

For decades, if not longer, political and social landscapes have been littered with phrases used to disparage or discredit people in what are commonly known as "culture wars." For example, the label of "PC" or "politically correct" is famously used by conservative critics to describe adherents to liberal points of view on various topics. The "P" of "PC" makes clear that what's being labeled is considered misguided, insincere, or both. Another example is the label of "right-wing nuts" famously used by critics on the ideological "left" to describe adherents to conservative points of view on various topics. The "nuts" makes clear that what's being labeled is considered irrational, hysterical, or both.

It's difficult to advance our understanding of the Growth Advantage Mindset by either using or ignoring these kinds of labels. After all, the words "political" and "nuts" were chosen precisely because they are *intended* as insults. Deliberate insults reinforce divisions while satisfying a desire to punish or retaliate. The "woke" label, however, may actually be useful to explore and claim together. This label is claimed by combatants on both sides of culture wars. It is used by some conservatives as a pejorative of liberal hyper-sensitivity to perceived inequities, while liberals claim it, describing conservatives, as ignorantly sleepwalking in the face of injustices. People who say they are neither totally conservative nor totally liberal on issues often are perplexed by the verbal battles and avoid the topics altogether to avoid the labels.

So, how does being "woke" relate to the Growth Advantage Mindset? First, let's agree that either ignoring or overreacting to what's happening in the present moment is not helpful. Second, let's agree that recognizing and working with unearned advantage is necessary to grow earned advantage. To one degree or another, you have "woken up" to points of view and experiences other than your own. You can't explore the elephant while sleepwalking or trapped in a nightmare. Expanding your Growth Advantage Mindset involves increasing your awareness of yourself, of others, and of the impact you have on others. RAIN can help you do that.

In the Natural Awareness of RAIN, we learned that labeling people without understanding them comes from the Fixed Advantage Mindset. There are conservative and there are liberal growth mindsets. There are conservative and there are liberal fixed mindsets. Politics do not make mindset. For the Growth Advantage Mindset, "woke" is about awareness – of self and others. Self-awareness recognizes if words like "woke" stimulate an insightful, empowered, assertive GAM response or a flight, fight, freeze, or appease a FAM reaction to perceived threats.

Politics do not make mindset.

Other-awareness is working to understand the experience of others, including having and not having unearned advantage – to see their part of the elephant. Self-on-other awareness is understanding the opportunity to grow earned advantage for all by reducing the take of unearned advantage. Understanding this interplay helps us realize that the GAM isn't related to being on the left or right but to being aware – of self, others, and self on others. People identified as conservatives may indeed hold a GAM and people identified as liberals may indeed hold a FAM. As we said, politics don't make or reflect a mindset. Instead, imagine if political debates and speeches weren't allowed to use labels to describe other people? Imagine if positions had to be explained instead of fit onto a bumper sticker or a tweet? How would it be different?

One significant opportunity in *Growing the Elephant*, particularly in an age of increasing polarization and yelling-at instead of speaking-with, is how each of us can see beyond the labels that cover up and ignore the vital and valuable differences of who we are and where we're from. In the Introduction, we mentioned the competitive advantages of contribution and innovation that come from increasing earned advantage. Another advantage, perhaps just as compelling, is the community and individual advantages of collaborative problem-solving and collective health and well-being.

Growing earned advantage – some practices

Growing earned advantage includes "paying forward" things like developing others through mentoring, coaching, and advocating, particularly and unapologetically *for* those with less unearned advantage and *by* those with more of it. Growing earned advantage doesn't happen by accident or overnight but by intentional action and day after day.

Reflection – growing earned advantages for two, please

Just as Maria had found with Alvin, you *grow* earned advantage when you *work with* it with another person. Center yourself for this exercise as you have for similar exercises. You may feel like a pro by now – pros know always to warm up.

Who have you developed through mentoring, coaching, or advocating for in the past? Who has developed you in the past? How similar to or different are they from you?

What has influenced to whom you offered development? What has influenced who you have asked for development?

Name someone different from you who would benefit from your support or development. Then, name someone different from you whose support or development would help you. Then, imagine talking to each of those persons about what you would offer and receive in such a relationship. How does that discussion go?

Set an intention for having this discussion. Decide the person, the timing, the place, the offer, and the ask. Meet your intention.

Asking for opportunity for earned advantage

Part of the GAM is seeing the abundance of earned advantage *opportunities*. While those with influence can create opportunities through mentoring, etc., those seeking them can stimulate the creation of opportunities as well. Yvonne thought about this and took a shot at it.

"Thanks for meeting with me, Robert. I've been thinking about my impact and career and would like to take it to the next level. You're really good at understanding what the executives are looking for – it's evident in our meetings. So, I was wondering – is that a skill or perspective you would consider mentoring with me? Even if just a few discussions?"

"Thanks, Yvonne! That's something I've learned over some years – and some mistakes! Sure, I'm open to that." A thought crossed Robert's mind, *I doubt Yvonne would do it the way I do it, but she wants to learn, so OK.* "Let's meet once a week for a few weeks?"

Something Robert didn't think about, but did notice, was how good it felt to be recognized for a skill and thought of as a teacher. Neither of them had thought consciously about something else they both instinctively knew – when we are asked for help for something in our power, most of us want to give it. Lastly, neither had recognized that Yvonne had enrolled Robert as an advocate for her performance and career through this agreement. By mentoring Yvonne, Robert now had a stake in her success. Robert raised that stake not long after by sharing with an executive that he was mentoring Yvonne in management presentations.

Yvonne could have asked someone else, but she went to the most skilled person she knew, regardless of unearned advantage. Robert accepted when he could have refused or delayed but, like most of us, he responded positively when asked to give something well within his ability to provide. Yvonne could have asked for many things – skill mentorship, ideation partner, access to his personal or professional networks, or even behavioral feedback. All of these are earned advantages that can be requested. They may not always be granted but, as Alvin said, "You rarely get anything (good) that you didn't ask for."

Increasing awareness – three kinds

We've talked about "awareness" at different points so far, especially in *recognizing* and *working with* advantage. In *growing* advantage, we dive a bit deeper into *awareness* and how it relates to each of these.

Often, we use "awareness" as we do "attention," just like we sometimes use "compassion" and "empathy" or "sympathy." But just as those terms are different, so are awareness and attention. Since we use the word "awareness" so much, it's useful to define it.

We "pay attention" because that's something we've been told to do most of our lives. As a student growing up, some of us heard "Pay attention!" a lot, mostly because our minds were wandering beyond the classroom or ahead to the weekend.

Paying attention narrows the focus to something specific and is essential to how we learn in school and succeed on task. Awareness, however, is different.

Think about how differently we use the words, at least in common English grammar. We "give," "direct," or "pay" attention, but we "are" (or "are not") aware. Attention is something we *do*; awareness is something we are simply supposed to *be*. While we are taught as children the many ways in which we should pay attention, we get little education about being aware. Paying attention to awareness – to be aware of awareness – is necessary to know what's actually happening in any given moment.

Self-awareness

We start with *self-awareness*, which is the accurate insight into what we are feeling, thinking, and doing in the present moment. Self-awareness is how we *recognize* and manage our relationships to unearned advantage. When we're self-aware, we can feel our reactions to what's happening and set intentions for how we want to respond. Self-awareness enables self-compassion. We know when to STOP – Stop, Take a Breath, Observe, and Proceed through self-awareness.

It is not a stretch to say that developing self-awareness is a life-long exercise. "I didn't mean that!" "I wish I'd said that!" happens when we're not self-aware. The need for self-awareness is one reason mindfulness has become the bright, shiny object of the last decade and why some members of our team took mindfulness training and have been reading up on it.[6]

---

[6] Chris Altizer, "Mindfulness: Performance, wellness, or fad?", *Strategic HR Review*, 2017;16(1): 24–31. https://doi.org/10.1108/SHR-10-2016-0093

Other-awareness

Self-awareness grounds our *other-awareness* – the accurate insight into what *others* are feeling, thinking, and doing in the present moment. Unless you live completely alone, knowing others, or other-awareness, is essential to function in business and community. MBA curricula standards like Robert Cialdini's *Psychology of Influence: The Psychology of Persuasion* and Roger Fisher and William Ury's *Getting to Yes* are business classics because other-awareness is a competitive advantage. That said, here, it's more than the negotiating tips, influencing hacks, and neurolinguistic tricks to get someone to do what you want them to do.

Other-awareness is how we *recognize* and *work with* advantage with others in the moment that counts – the present moment. Through other-awareness, we can extend from sympathy to empathy and relate to the experience of others with less judgment and more compassion. Through other-awareness, we can make it RAIN – Recognize, Accept, Investigate with Natural Awareness what is happening in both ourselves and others.

Self-on-other awareness

Self-awareness and other-awareness enable a third type of awareness, *self-on-other awareness*.[7] This awareness is our real-time insight into how *our* feelings, thoughts, and behaviors impact *others* in the moment. This level of understanding allows us to RAIN and then choose what we are doing in the moment and see its impact. When we do that, we can recalibrate how we respond in each moment to accomplish what we set out to accomplish. Through self-on-other awareness,

---

[7] Chris Altizer, "Self? Other? Self-on-Other?" *LinkedIn*, December 6, 2021. Available from www.linkedin.com/pulse/self-other-self-on-other-chris-altizer-ma-mba/ [accessed May 5, 2022].

we can tell if our intentions are being met and if our actions are having the impact we intended.

If it's difficult enough to increase self- and other-awareness, how can we cultivate this third kind?

Self-on-other awareness – a cycle

As we said, self-on-other (SOO) awareness is the real-time insight into how one's feelings, thoughts, and behaviors impact others in the present moment enabling recalibration to achieve intention. Through SOO awareness, I can tell if my intentions are being met and if my actions have the impact I intended. We all think we do this in most interactions. To one degree or another, we do. But practicing it when we're exploring the elephant with others is not easy.

First, SOO awareness builds on both self- and other-awareness. By recognizing and working with advantage, you've been building your own awareness.

On any given day, we can all struggle to flow through the entire cycle, and most of us tend to cut the cycle short when we are highly focused or stressed. This is true for all of us. It's especially true for leaders.

My Self
- Lived Experiences
- Natural Traits
- Intentions

My Response
- Perception
- Interpretation
- Adapt Behaviors

My Behavior
- Thought/Feeling
- Verbal/Non-Verbal
- Actions/Inactions

Others' Response
- Perception
- Interpretation
- Response behavior

However one achieves power of position, earned or unearned, that power becomes its own tailwind. It probably doesn't surprise you that people with more power often have blind spots in seeing the impact they have on people with less power.[8] It probably also doesn't surprise you that research shows that when people feel powerful, they believe more in what they think.[9] When you consider that leaders are typically more ambitious than others to begin with, you can see how power can propel itself![10] Do you recall exploring how those with tailwinds don't notice them? Experts Ben Fuchs, Megan Reitz, and John Higgins describe how leaders can have *advantage blindness* – you don't notice a life of advantage; it's just normal.[11] Self-on-other awareness is important and yet challenging for all of us. It's doubly so for leaders.

For all of us, leaders and followers (and each of us are both), intentionally moving through the entire cycle increases the odds of sustaining awareness and growing opportunities for earned advantage. Here's how it works.

• **My Self – self-awareness**
This cycle begins with My Self. This includes all of who you are and where you're from and your intentions. Most of us

---

[8] Robert B. Shaw, *Leadership Blindspots: How Successful Leaders Identify and Overcome the Weaknesses That Matter.* Jossey-Bass, 2014.

[9] Pablo Briñol, Richard E. Petty, Carmen Valle, Derek D. Rucker, and Alberto Becerra, "The effects of message recipients' power before and after persuasion: A self-validation analysis." *Journal of Personality and Social Psychology*, 2007;93(6): 1040–1053. https://doi.org/10.1037/0022-3514.93.6.1040

[10] Ashley Bell Jones, Ryne A. Sherman, and Robert T. Hogan, "Where is ambition in factor models of personality?" *Personality and Individual Differences*, 2017;106: 26–31, https://doi.org/10.1016/j.paid.2016.09.057

[11] Ben Fuchs, Megan Reitz, and John Higgins, "Do you have advantage blindness?", *Harvard Business Review*, April 10, 2018. Available from https://hbr.org/2018/04/do-you-have-advantage-blindness [accessed May 5, 2022].

start with self-awareness, at least of what we are thinking if not always what we are feeling. For some, particularly the self-centered or narcissists (who aren't likely reading this), it starts and ends there. We've written a lot about who you are, but for SOO awareness we focus on lived experiences, natural traits, and intentions.

Earlier, we wrote about the GAM of **lived experience** (pp. 63–66) and how valuable it is for you to know your lived experiences for what they actually were and realize that yours are not always shared by everyone else. While you can't know everyone else's, you can be aware that others have different experiences just as "real" as yours, including those shaped by earned and unearned advantages.

Your **natural traits**, including all of who you are and where you're from, including your personality and talents, contribute to your self. Knowing your natural tendencies, particularly under stress, grounds you when it gets uncomfortable.

Finally, as Alvin had learned, **intentions** – what you want for what purpose – reflects who you are and intend to be. The groundwork of My Self – lived experiences, natural traits, and intentions – is all in place by design (or happenstance), and it shapes My Behavior – what you think, say, and do.

- **My Behavior – more self-awareness**

We break My Behavior into **thoughts/feelings**, **verbal/non-verbal**, and **action/inaction**. As human beings, we each have thoughts and feelings. Yvonne reflected, "Sometimes my head and heart just don't agree!" What you think and feel may feel different and even conflicted at times, but they are blended and each influences the other.

Then there's **verbal/non-verbal** – what's said, what's not said, and the power of physical expression. Words count – just as timing, tone, and energy count and should support intention. What we choose not to say, out of discretion or from fear, also counts. My Behavior also includes eye contact, physical distance, posture, etc. You may know or be someone who notices the "energy" in a room – tense, relaxed, anxious. Do you notice? Do you know what you're contributing to that energy, whatever it is?

While speech is a behavior, **action/inaction** converts words into deeds, ideally aligned to intention. When you get to the point of doing or not-doing – for whatever reasons – it still has to do with self-awareness. What you thought about doing was interesting (maybe), what you did or didn't do was relevant. Action/inaction is what is perceived by others that results in their reaction and gets to the next step – Others' Response.

- **Others' Response – other-awareness**

How often are you surprised by how someone responds to you? Do you find yourself sometimes having to explain yourself, "That's not what I meant..."? When this happens, we often wonder, "What's WRONG with that person?" as if they didn't get it. "Of COURSE I didn't mean that...!" as if your intentions were obvious to anyone paying attention. But when you miss a cue, you're missing Others' Response, you're missing other-awareness.

Other-awareness occurs when you allow enough of your attention to shift from what you're saying or doing to the other person's **perception**, **interpretation**, and **response behavior** in that moment. It's not easy to cycle from Self to Other, especially in difficult situations, including recognizing and working with unearned advantage. Here again, STOP is helpful. In this case, to shift to Others' Response:

- Stop – pause and shift your attention back one step to see what's actually going on. This isn't running away and certainly not hiding – stepping back is not standing by.

- Take a slow, deep breath. In difficult situations, your stress-response breathing – shallow, rapid – prepares you to fight, fly, freeze, or appease reflexively. You may choose one of these at some point; just don't trip into it by reflex.
- Observe – how that person(s) is reacting to your behavior – as well as to the subject at hand. Recognize that you may not know how you are perceived or if your intentions are accurately interpreted. Pay attention to their response – spoken and unspoken, action and inaction.
- Proceed – to My Response.

- **My Response – SOO awareness at work**

Your response, and your SOO awareness, begins with your **perception** and **interpretation** from your Others' Awareness. From that, you may realize you're being misunderstood for reasons that have nothing to do with you. Perhaps this has come up at a difficult time, or the other person is frustrated with having to tell a story again or anxious about saying what they really feel. Your considered response, or **Adapt Behavior**, in this case, is to reconsider time, place, or priority. You're not changing your intention, just your approach.

Or maybe they are resisting or avoiding your intention. In this case, your Adapt Behavior may be to reframe to account for reasons for resistance. If you don't know those reasons, your Adapt Behavior is to inquire rather than ignore or assume. A particular challenge for those with unearned advantages is to inquire without conveying skepticism of the other's experience. A particular challenge for those with less unearned advantage is to hear the inquiry without assuming disbelief.

Or it could be that you're simply not getting it right. Your willingness to accept that possibility will cycle your awareness back to My Self and My Behaviors. Are your lived experiences or natural traits limiting your awareness of unearned advantage? Are your intentions clear? Are you giving mixed signals? The faster you open yourself to these possibilities, the more efficiently and effectively you can Adapt Behavior. The more efficiently and effectively you Adapt Behavior, the more likely you will achieve my intention.

- **Practice Makes Better (there is no perfect)**

Similar to how mindsets can naturally be more or less growth, awareness comes more naturally to some than others. SOO awareness involves humility and empathy as well as confidence and a desire to have it. SOO awareness involves accepting that you may be wrong – not just sometimes, but this time. It involves understanding how others are feeling and caring enough to modify your approach. It involves being calm and confident enough to stay in the mix without fighting, flighting, freezing, or appeasing. It involves having purpose and courage because you want to make a difference.

Keep in mind that it begins with My Self. Your lived experiences and natural traits shape you – but you are more than their sum, and the power of intention is key. Cycling awareness through self, others, and back to self informs who you are. With practice, it strengthens the growth mindset that grows the elephant.

Through self-awareness, you can recognize your sources of unearned advantage. Through working with awareness, you can focus on other-awareness to guide your intentions and compassion. Then, when you put your intentions to work at *growing* advantage, you let your self-on-other awareness inform if you're hitting or missing the mark – and adjust.

When you start to explore different parts of the elephant, you're certainly going to be less than perfect! But when you let your self-on-other awareness inform you, you can better know if your intention is being met and better navigate the trunk, legs, and other parts of the elephant.

Awareness of self, others, and self-on-others allows us to more *accurately* see what is happening in the moment in which it's happening, which is key to *growing* earned advantage.

Increasing awareness?

To some degree, awareness of self, others, and self-on-others is natural and intuitive. That said, nature and experience play roles, and some people are more intuitively aware than others. You may know or be that person who can sense the mood in a room. You may know or be the one who can't catch a clue. The good news – everyone can increase it. The better news – you've already been doing it!

Just like our team members, each time you muster up the courage to explore a new part of the elephant, you increase awareness. Each time you pause to breathe, reflect, set an intention, STOP, or RAIN, you increase awareness. When you explore challenging questions and sit with the answers, you increase awareness. Like muscles, mindset, and intentions, awareness expands and grows stronger with work.

By getting to this point in this book, you have almost certainly increased your awareness and informed your mindset. Like Maria, you could also increase awareness through formal training in mindfulness, compassion, or similar programs. Whatever you do from here, you've grown your mind as well as opportunities for earned advantage. Another phrase from MBSR creator Jon Kabat-Zinn is, "Wherever you go, there you are." Well, here you are. Once you've begun growing earned advantage, you may find yourself getting better with practice!

GAM leadership – and followership

Whatever role you have in life, you are both a leader and a follower. You may lead only yourself, or a family, or a community, or an organization. You may follow your heart or intuition, a loved one, or a leader in your community or organization. There is a Growth Advantage Mindset for both leaders and followers. How do they grow earned advantage?

Leaders can grow earned advantage beyond their personal sphere of influence into their professional sphere of influence. They can review the formal rules, policies, and procedures in their world as well as informal norms, behaviors, and attitudes. These reviews can be just as challenging as the personal reflections in *recognizing*, *working with*, and *growing* earned advantage! Believe it or not, examining workplace or community rules and norms also benefits from practices of breath, reflection, intention setting, STOP, and RAIN. The recent COVID-19 pandemic, and implications that it carried forward, provides several examples:

- During COVID-19, Robert rushed to establish work-from-home rules that seemed to make sense and be fair. He didn't pause long enough to realize that, depending on where they are from, employees with less unearned advantage didn't have suitable computers or internet access at home. "I wanted to give people options," he said. "It wasn't until someone brought it up that we modified the policy to supply the hardware and mobile hotspots for those who didn't have access."

- While Alvin had anticipated the tech issues that Robert had missed, he also had a COVID-related miss. "My employee kept being late for work so we had to dock her pay. It turns out she didn't want to tell us that her bus routes to work were jammed up for a lack of drivers. When I asked and she told me, I offered more flexible hours – that helped."

- Yvonne had been holding Zoom meetings and was getting a bit annoyed by some people keeping cameras off and mics muted. "I realized I was creating a story in my head about these people," she said. "Finally, I asked one person why he was doing that. I hadn't realized he shared caregiver duties with his partner and he felt that was the best way to reduce background noise and commotion. After that, I opened each meeting inviting people to use chat and emoticons if they needed to be off camera."

As you read these, you probably realized these examples are not just about COVID. They are about the mindset around rules and norms. Whether dealing with formal or informal rules, having a growth mindset helps formal and informal leaders be open to learning and adapting how they lead to grow opportunities for earned advantage. Sometimes, the easiest way to learn and adapt is to ask "why," and then be willing to listen closely.

Followers can also grow earned advantage in many ways, including in choosing who to follow. Remember, wherever you go, there you are. When you follow, you end up where the leader goes. Followership can also support – or detract from – growing and fairly distributing earned advantage opportunities. In the 21st century, this has gone

beyond (but still includes) politics, religion, and employment to include preferred and "liked" presences on social
media, your favorite information sources, and your product loyalty. It includes choices we each make about what
and how we support and what and how we protest. All
of these lend our followership to leadership. All of these
begin with mindset.

The Growth Advantage Mindset expands opportunities for earned advantage. However, these opportunities
can also be taken or lost when Fixed Advantage Mindsets
successfully promote notions of competition over cooperation, or aggression, appeasement, and avoidance over assertive engagement, as well as zero-sum instead of abundance.
The opportunity, or obligation, of GAM leaders is to apply
the powers of position and assertively challenge the FAM.
Likewise, the opportunity, or obligation, of GAM followers is to make their followership decisions with intent and
accountability rather than from habit or convenience. Life
in the 21st century provides several examples:

- Maria's family and friends relied on one media channel for news and information. "Talking about politics
  these days is hard enough as it is. Who has the time
  to read twenty different points of view and vet every
  single statement for accuracy?" Maria followed a particular source of information out of convenience and
  alignment with her views. She reflected, "I suppose I
  could listen to another point of view sometimes – it's
  not like it's hard to know which channel is pushing
  which narrative!"
- Maria's mother was a big supporter of one particular
  community leader. "If he says it, I believe it," she exclaimed to Maria. Maria reflected that some of her
  work colleagues felt the same way about their CEO.

"Loyalty to a leader is important," Maria thought. She was a bit surprised one day, however, when that CEO openly thanked and praised a subordinate for expressing and holding a disagreement on a particular decision. At home, her mother was surprised when her community leader lost his position due to a favoritism scandal. "I guess we were both surprised," Maria said. "I guess there's loyalty and then there's blind loyalty!"

The nature of the GAM is to see the entire elephant and expand opportunities for earned advantage. The nature of the FAM is to be fixed and declare the elephant to be no more than what it can see. These will inevitably come into conflict. GAM leaders and followers lead by facing these conflicts with compassion for self and others.

They also know that fixed mindsets are not grown by attacking or berating those with them but by increasingly calling in, rather than exclusively calling out. We can all lead – from in front or from behind. But we can't lead from the stands. We can't grow earned advantage by watching and waiting or attacking or baiting. Maria adopted a famous phrase that our resilient little team now bandies about when they develop new approaches for difficult challenges, "Hope is not a strategy!" Growing earned advantage happens when we approach the elephant with courage and intention. Hoping it will grow by itself isn't a strategy.

GAM leadership in action – Robert explores "dimensions of power"

As Robert was reflecting on what he'd been learning about growing opportunities for earned advantage, he began thinking about what he would bring back to the organization he led. "I've learned some things I can do as a person to make things better for me and those I work with, for sure. But I'm wondering, what can I take back to the place where I'm in charge? I want to get more diversity of perspectives, make the place more inclusive, and ensure more equitable outcomes – but how?"

By asking himself the question, Robert was well on his way toward developing answers. He recalls an insight provided during a leadership development session about DEI *Dimensions of Power©*. It's a framework for understanding how the transformation to achieve more diversity, equity, and inclusion in organizations requires sharing some of the power involved in setting priorities, seeking diverse perspectives, and aiming for inclusive representation.

DEI Dimensions of Power

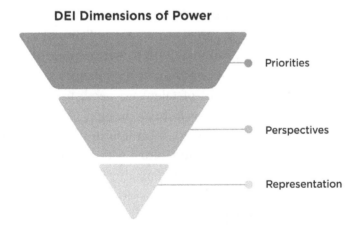

Priorities

Perspectives

Representation

Robert assessed his own power as both a business and a community leader. He is CEO of a health services company and is also board chair of a regional foundation responsible for disbursing philanthropic funds to community organizations committed to improving health, education, and wealth generation. "I don't have absolute power, but I have more influence than anyone else over what happens, why it happens, and when and how." Using a Growth Advantage Mindset, Robert set his intentions on doing what he could in his unique leadership roles.

Aiming for inclusive representation – pausing to consider a different approach

He imagined a better way, starting with what seemed the easiest dimension of power to influence: increasing the representation of underrepresented groups. As CEO of his company, he thought about adjusting policies and practices regarding employment and contracting. Researchers have found that most organizations increase their effectiveness when their teams are powered by a diversity of perspectives that come from diversity in terms of race, ethnicity, age, and gender – who you are and where you're from. "I won't try to change the make-up of our team or our policies and practices all at once, but I can take steps to start requesting data and having team discussions about a few changes we could make to improve the kind of talent we need, to keep our competitive advantage." As Robert thought more about the market his company served, it hit him in the face. "Our market demographic is shifting, along with its needs! If we have more diversity in our decision-making jobs, the research shows we'll make more informed decisions. If we have more diversity in our service-provider jobs, the research shows our customers will feel better served!"

As chairman of the board of the Foundation, Robert focused on diverse representation on the board. "My personal and professional contacts may mostly be a lot like me, but I know I can get people to return my phone calls when I reach out to find people who are NOT a lot like me."

Seeking diverse perspectives – listening more before finalizing decisions

As Robert thought about diversity of decision-makers, he became more ambitious. He thought about opportunities to engage more people with less unearned advantage in organizational decision making. "I might not have the representation of people from diverse backgrounds and perspectives that I want right away at my company," he thought, "But there's no reason why I can't make sure the decision-makers we have right now are equipped and committed to making the progress we need to make. I'll make sure they know what's expected of them, that they have the tools and training they need, and that we increase our understanding about how we can all do better if we go out there and find people who can help us. If we don't have the mindsets and channels for listening and learning from people we have excluded, then we'll explore ways to change both." Robert had begun to see the link between increasing earned advantage and competitive advantage. "The way we market our products – or even the products themselves – haven't kept pace with our changing customers. Time to fix that."

Robert also considered how he can influence decision making as the board chair at the Foundation. "It's about including underrepresented groups in our decision making, especially to help the board and staff understand what matters most to the people in the communities we aim to support." Robert also realized there was a scary part of the elephant they would have to explore. "I suppose we'll be opening ourselves up to criticism and feedback we'd rather not hear. And some of the ideas community members offer will be feasible and some will not. But we have got to practice listening, to stop always trying to be the 'know it alls.' Even for those solutions that we can't or wouldn't do, our leadership team might listen and learn things we really need to know. Recent news about hate and courageous actions sure have shown me that there are lots of challenges out there, and maybe even more solutions in our communities if we are more inclusive."

Robert recognized a lesson that many organizations had learned through increasing representation and cultivating affinity groups – you get a more informed perspective when you organize seeking it. By engaging those with less unearned advantage in dialogue and problem-solving, he would be sharing that dimension of power. "I don't know exactly how our decision making will change, but I do know the quality of our leadership will improve because we'll ask more important questions – questions that matter to more people and that give us a chance at improving what we do."

Setting organizational priorities – leveraging the power of messaging, people, and money

Finally, Robert considered the highest and most consequential dimension of power sharing: setting organizational priorities. "As a leader, I've always had to set priorities around communications, budgeting, and HR policy stuff – not exactly earth-shattering. But I've come to see the impact these can make on my team's efforts to expand opportunities and help our team outperform our competitors." Robert thought about ways he could use his most powerful tools. He could use his voice specifically to articulate how holding a Growth Advantage Mindset can advance the performance of an organization. He had seen how top leaders use their first-person messaging to signal top priorities for the organization. "I can be sure to state my intentions to increase diversity, equity, and inclusion in my statements to the board, staff, and external partners as well as in my presentations, blogs, and social media posts. One thing I realize for sure is that if I fail to find opportunities to voice my intentions – especially knowing so much more about the inequality of opportunity – then my silence is consent."

In addition, Robert could focus on increasing the GAM with his leaders who most influence financial and human capital to develop and execute plans that align resources with measurable outcomes suited to the organization's business model. He remembered Alvin's counsel on intention setting, so he set one for himself and his company. "For the upcoming cycle, we will pressure test and validate our budgets and people plans with a test: how, by how much, and by when will these plans advance our company objectives for diversity, inclusion, and equity?" Without losing a beat, he added, "And we will pressure test each DEI objective by linking each with a measurable outcome like customer retention, product innovation, and employee engagement."

The same might be true at the Foundation. "When we are providing strategic direction to our executive director, I can task our board committees to spend more time analyzing and incorporating what we learned from listening more intentionally to people in our communities. I know we can be smarter about how we approve strategy, metrics, and budgets. Even if we have to take steps that are more measured than some people will want, we'll set a path and adjust as we learn."

"For the company and the Foundation board that I lead, I want my intentions to be reflected in every part of the organization, and I want those intentions to show up well after I am no longer the leader. I want every team member to decide they will try to BE different leaders and followers.

Then, maybe the way we ACT – for the long haul – will look different too."

Robert has recognized a lesson that continues to be learned by leaders in every sector – stakeholders are increasingly expecting to be engaged in solving the challenges they face. Whether in business, the charitable sector, the public sector, or higher education, the role of leaders is to include more people in the dimensions of power, which expands opportunities for earned advantage. Expanding inclusion in dimensions of power creates shared purpose and accountability – evolving a group of people into a team.

Research has shown that well-managed diverse teams outperform homogeneous teams.[12] The same research also shows that homogeneous teams outperform poorly managed diverse teams. Well-managed diverse teams thrive, while non-diverse teams (regardless of management) survive. The key difference? Leadership. Whether customers or employees, shareholders or taxpayers, educators or students, civil servants or citizens, the world has become too small and too fast to limit the opportunity to engage in problem-solving to leaders.

Chapter summary

In this chapter, you've focused on *growing* earned advantage, our goal for the elephant in the room. You've gone through the processes of *recognizing* and *working with* advantage and in this chapter addressed some of the difficult challenges to *growing* advantage – biases, baggage, and micro-aggressions. "Growing pains" are a function of stretching our abilities

---

[12] J. J. Distefano and M. L. Maznevski, "Creating value with diverse teams in global management," *Organizational Dynamics*, 2000;29(1): 45–63. https://doi.org/10.1016/S0090-2616(00)00012-7

and perspectives, just like working out in the gym strains and slightly tears muscles to grow them. If you found this chapter challenging, you're in the right company.

You also learned how to *grow* advantage by RAINing, supporting others, and increasing your awareness. If the going gets tough, remember you've been introduced to your "window of tolerance" and reminded of your option to STOP whenever you need to so you can go again.

Finally, you've explored GAM leadership and followership. Whether you lead or follow (and most of us do both), you have opportunities to grow opportunities for earned advantage through your intentional choices. In whatever circumstance you lead, you can grow opportunities by exploring dimensions of power to accelerate, decide, and prioritize.

By *growing* earned advantage, you're meeting the intention for this book and this work! Doing this in your daily life will improve the lives of those around you in the many situations and roles you provide either leadership or followership. You may surprise yourself with how it improves your life, as well.

Growing earned advantage reflections

Leadership reflection

Whether in your family, community, workplace, society, or just for yourself – you provide leadership. Taking time to settle and reflect on this chapter, consider:

1. How can you as a leader create the conditions for growing earned advantage? How can you make

it RAIN in your daily interactions with others –
those similar to and different from who you are
and where you're from? To whom can you extend
the benefit of the doubt to increase opportunities
for earned advantage?

2. As you explore creating those conditions, how
can you increase your awareness of the impact of
your words and behaviors on others? Who can you
enlist to expand your self-on-other awareness?

3. What tangible, observable steps can you take in
sharing dimensions of power? With whom and how
can you be inclusive of who is in the room, who has
"the D" of decisions, and what is truly important?

4. What is the most valuable lesson for you in this
chapter? How can you optimize and maximize
that value?

Followership reflection

Whether in your family, community, workplace, society, or just for yourself – you contribute to leadership by lending your followership. Taking time to settle and reflect on this chapter, consider:

1. To whom, what, and where do you currently lend your followership? Do you lend it intentionally or by habit? Does it contribute to a growth or fixed mindset?
2. How can you as a faithful follower cultivate the conditions for growing earned advantage? How can you make it RAIN and increase your awareness in your daily interactions with others – those similar to and different from who you are and where you're from?
3. What tangible, observable steps can you take in asking for or sharing opportunities for earned advantage? Into what rooms can you bring your followership, give input to "the D" of decisions, and inform what is truly important?
4. What is the most valuable lesson for you in this chapter? How can you optimize and maximize that value?

This chapter included the most challenging, the most scary, parts of the elephant. Which of the practices in this chapter came more easily to you? Did any come with difficulty? Were any beyond what you wanted or felt you could do? Consider revisiting these at different times and settings. Then, as your comfort working with them increases, consider discussing your experiences with others. Growing earned advantage happens when you engage others!

Chapter 4: Tusks, trumpets, legs, and other tails

Time to apply the practice

As we researched, wrote, and discussed this book with others, we found ourselves exploring many different parts of the elephant – some in our own experience and some beyond it. While we (Gloria and Chris) each have distinctly different lived experiences and ways of analyzing and understanding them, we recognize there are many ways to take it all in, make sense of it, and do something with it.

The following few stories are shared experiences adapted from real-life stories. These include situations without conclusions or tidy endings – just like real life. Some of them seemed to either fit into more than one chapter or not clearly into any of them. But they were compelling enough for us to include them and invite your additional thought, perhaps additional discussion, and perhaps even additional action.

At the end of each story is a "For reflection" exercise. Consider writing down what thoughts or feelings occur to you as you reflect on the story and respond to the questions. As with every story, there is plenty of detail and information you don't have – but you probably won't need. If you decide you do, feel free to fill in your own blanks and then start making your mental or written notes.

Justin and Dudley – two strong legs of the elephant

"What doesn't kill you..."

Justin had had enough. "I'm a successful businessman in America. I've served my country, earned my education, and made sacrifices to get where I am. Yes, I'm Black – and I've flown into headwinds so strong you can barely keep your eyes open. BUT I've had to get better and be stronger than others to get there, and I have. I value self-reliance and equality of opportunity, but all this self-reflection and getting-in-touch-with-my-feelings business is a waste. I do what I can to help anyone who deserves it – whoever they are or wherever they're from."

There is a popular ethos that, to paraphrase the philosopher Friedrich Nietzsche, what doesn't kill you makes you stronger. If that were true, those without unearned advantages would be ruling the world, or at least be healthier. Justin knows the data is clear that minority groups experience higher rates of disease, death, along with other negative health outcomes.[1] Justin is not alone in feeling a sense of pride in his achievements despite having fewer unearned advantages. He also isn't alone in avoiding reflecting on his experience – "touchy-feely" isn't his thing. "It is what it is," Justin says. "What's the point of talking about what can't be changed?"

Enough of the snowflakes

Dudley had also had enough. "I'm a hard-working, high-school-educated, store supervisor in a small, church-going community. If I'm lucky, I won't lose what I have

---

[1] Centers for Disease Control and Prevention, "Health equity," 2021. Available from www.cdc.gov/healthequity/racism-disparities/index.html [accessed May 5, 2022].

earned. Yes, I'm as White, Christian, straight, able, etc., as Robert – I'm even taller! Now, tell me how all these unearned advantages add up for me? Who in my town am I growing earned advantage for? Seems to me that we're all in the exact same boat but not everybody is rowing! Am I supposed to be growing earned advantage for some snowflake – whoever they are or wherever they are from – looking for a leg-up when I'm lucky to provide for my family?"

Justin and Dudley have more in common than meets the eye. Both value hard work, persistence, and a values-guided life. Both share values of individual responsibility and resilience. Justin's life experience is that it's harder to be financially and professionally successful and Black in America – but possible. Dudley's life experience is that, despite his unearned advantages and hard work, financial and professional stability seem almost out of reach. Justin has a sense that the "American Dream" once denied to Black people in America is possible but limited, while Dudley has a sense that the "American Dream" once available to White people in America is being withheld or unfairly redistributed.

You can replace Justin and Dudley with any combination of who you are and where you're from. You might even be one or both of them.

For reflection

Have you explored this part of the elephant? What practices from this book would you suggest to Justin? How about Dudley? What does compassion look like in practice for these men? How might their values be a basis for intention setting?

The tusk and the trumpet – a (mostly) true story

Robert's niece, Susan, and Yvonne's sister, Janet, are both educators and have known each other for a few years. During COVID, their school held a virtual DEI session intended to stimulate workplace dialogue and understanding of different experiences of privilege and justice. During the session, Janet began sharing her experiences. One of them was very difficult to talk about. She had proudly taken the signing-bonus check from her new employer to open an account, only to be refused under suspicion of fraud (true story, but not this story).[2] Susan, who generally avoided discussions of race, at least outside her family, didn't understand how any bank could do such a thing. Susan asked, "How did that happen?"

Janet heard the question, but what she mostly heard was, "did that happen?" What Susan didn't know was that Janet was sharing an experience she had shared many times before – but was ignored or glossed over as "the exception." What Susan didn't anticipate was Janet's deep-seated frustration with having to tell the story – again – without receiving understanding or hope of tangible action. Susan thought, "I didn't do that! I'd never do that! But I feel like if I don't say something, Janet will think I'm OK with what happened? Maybe I'll apologize that she had that experience."

Susan's apology landed with a thud. "I'm not asking for an apology," Janet replied. "I'm so tired of telling the same story, and in these sessions it seems I'm always encouraged

---

[2] Antonio Planas, "Black doctor sues JPMorgan Chase alleging she was refused service at Texas branch because of race," *NBC News*, February 3, 2022. Available from www.nbcnews.com/news/us-news/black-doctor-sues-jpmorgan-chase-alleging-was-refused-service-texas-br-rcna14753 [accessed May 5, 2022].

to speak up. Yet, I keep getting the same result – nothing changes! I feel like I'm going insane!"

After a moment of really awkward silence, Susan muted herself. "I don't know what I'm supposed to say! I don't think I'll say anything else – ever." Janet's reaction was, ironically, the same. "Either I can't explain it or they can't understand it – or both. I'm done."

For reflection

Have you explored this part of the elephant? What practices or reflections from this book would you suggest to Susan? To Janet? What can one do when it just seems too hot to stay engaged? What is possible for Susan and Janet if they can stay in the moment with each other?

Maria's and Idell's search for common ground

At a conference that convened leaders in business, philanthropy, and community organizations interested in improving outcomes for everyone in health, education, the environment, and financial security, Maria meets Idell. She is director of a nonprofit providing human services to children and families. At a plenary session, Maria stood to share her enthusiasm about a project she recently joined that aims to build commercial centers in several rural communities, including one inhabited by the Haliwa Saponi tribe in North Carolina. She smilingly threw out statistics about expected tax revenues to the state, milestone dates, and other outcomes, while Idell felt her face turning hot. She looked around the room observing people taking notes, other people checking emails on their phones, and she thought, "I've got to speak up or I will explode." When Maria finished, Idell asked for the roaming microphone. "I need to say something. Something that feels important and I don't know exactly why, but this is hard, my hands are trembling and I ask for your patience." People in the room turned to Idell. "That community, those Haliwa Saponi people you referred to, Maria, they are my family; a band who lived in North Carolina since the early 1700s. I am really angry." Maria felt eyes on her.

> *"I am not angry that you, Maria, are working on this project. The aims are good. But I am angry now – actually, quite often, because I know all too well why it's even necessary for outsiders to come and try at some kind of economic development in that place. I know why it's necessary for me and other nonprofit leaders to scratch around for dollars to try to support whole communities living there below the poverty line. It's because the Haliwa Saponi, who were never enslaved, had our most fertile land confiscated legally by big timber companies. It was land we could have continued cultivating to be self-sustaining in every way. And I know too well how we had our federal tribal designation denied us by some clever scoundrels who devised a loophole to make sure we'd never be entitled to resources owed to other tribes. I gotta say this to you all even though it feels like someone is choking me while I talk. It's me bearing witness I guess – so this conversation is more than us just thinking about performance metrics and budgets. I've spent most of my career deciding to convert this anger into something positive, something that changes situations for people who have been treated unfairly for generations. But it gets hard."*

Idell stood silent. "I really hope I can find a way to keep doing this community work. It's taking a toll, being expected to show up everyday being calm and being whatever 'objective' means; because, really, I sometimes struggle to imagine that those of you here who are not of color seriously have to deal with all this hurt. I know why I am here. I wonder if you do."

Maria wanted to cry for Idell, and for herself too. "Here I am trying to do good. No, I don't feel the personal pain Idell is telling us about, but I'm trying. I think both of us are wondering if this is worth it? The issues are so complicated." Maria looked around the room to see if others were struggling like her. She began to reflect in the quiet room. "Honestly, I haven't had to think a lot about all these complications because I don't have to deal with being treated differently all the time. No accent, no color. Less bias. It's just the truth." She recalled a comment Alvin made to her in that DEI session a few months ago. "It's just a matter of time before you realize how big a luxury it is to be able to choose to withhold your identity as a Latina immigrant – just as I sometimes choose about my sexual identity." "It sure doesn't feel like a luxury today," she thought. "I feel like people in this room assume I don't know enough to be an ally, and worse, that I don't care as much as I should. Her mind turned back to Idell again. "What do I say to Idell when I see her one on one? Heck, what do I say to myself about how in the world I get the energy to keep learning and having these conversations without feeling as overwhelmed as I feel right now? When I set my intentions on being an ally with others on diversity, equity, and inclusion, I sure didn't think I was signing up for this!"

For reflection

This case may present unfamiliar facts if who you are and where you're from isn't indigenous to wherever you live, North America in this case. Idell is a new character in our story, but her experience is as real as those you have come to know.

Notice Maria's sense of overwhelm at being confronted by facts outside of her lived experience. Are the feelings Idell is sharing also outside Maria's lived experience? Imagine yourself to be Maria – what do you have in common with Idell? What can you share one on one to begin to recognize and work with Idell's experience? How can you grow earned advantage with Idell? What can you do to resource yourself and your intentions to be an ally?

Notice Idell's sense of overwhelm at sharing the frustrations of her lived experiences. Have you had the experience of sharing a challenging experience or perception that few others have had? Imagine yourself to be Idell – what do you have in common with Maria? Even if it seems you have the fewest unearned advantages, how can you engage allies to recognize and work with those with so few? What can you do to resource yourself and your intentions to grow earned advantage?

The elephant in my backyard – Robert and Jim

Robert and Jim have been close friends for decades. "I pretty much know what he's going to say before he says it," Robert said. "And vice-versa, buddy!" Jim replies. These men are similar in almost every measure of who you are and where you're from. Over the last few years, however, their views on matters of social justice and inequality have parted ways. "I love the guy," Jim said, "but the whole woke thing has Robert by the throat. I think he's feeling guilty for who he is and he's thinking about it all too much. It seems to me he's got an excuse for anything wrong that non-White people do and it always seems to be White people's fault. We've gotten to where we just agree not to talk about it – which kind of sucks."

Robert felt the same discomfort that Jim felt – though for different reasons. "Not only do I like Jim, but I have always respected him," Robert said. "It's been a tough slog over a few years for me to recognize and work with my unearned advantage but I feel like I'm better for it – and maybe have helped some others be better! Sometimes Jim makes cracks about women or people of color – and frankly, I used to, too. I can tell he doesn't get where I am on all of it now, but I want to meet Jim where he is. I'm not trying to change him, but I do want him to understand where I am now. I'm just not sure how to do that without fracturing our friendship."

For reflection

Have you explored this part of the elephant? What practices from this book or from your lived experience would you suggest Robert consider? What are his options to "meet Jim where he is" with awareness? As so many families find, there are some subjects, some elephants in the room, that are best left ignored for the sake of navigating short family gatherings or occasional phone or video calls. But Robert wants to keep his friendship with Jim as close as it's been with an intention to share what he's learned. Can he? How?

How about Jim? He knows how Robert feels but feels his friend has been swept along by an agenda. Might Jim, out of respect for Robert, read this book? Even reading it through a skeptical lens, what might he gain from it? Imagine what might their conversation after reading it be like? What's the best possible outcome? What's the worst? What's likely?

Imagine you are sitting next to Jim on a long flight and that he shares his experience with Robert with you (this might seem far-fetched, but less-likely discussions happen every day). What would you listen for? What might you ask him? What might you share with him? If you relate to Jim, what do you make of all this?

Chapter 5: What next?

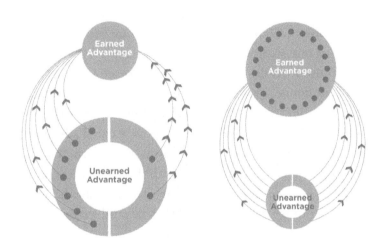

Growing earned advantage – the fertilizer of courage

Throughout this book, you have explored different parts of the elephant. Some have been familiar, and some very uncomfortable. Opportunities for earned advantage grow rapidly when you shrink the share taken by unearned advantage and actively cultivate earned advantage. As we've said from the start, this is hard work and it requires courage to explore, whether alone or with others. Each of our characters has headwinds to face, though not equally. For those with less unearned advantage, the courage needed is to face the headwinds each moment and day. The exhaustion of flying into the headwinds becomes as challenging as the fact that the headwinds exist. Facing unearned advantage when it's not yours is frustrating and threatening on many levels. But what courage is needed for those with unearned advantages?

As Robert realized, with some irony, facing unearned advantage when it's yours also requires courage. That courage helped Robert avoid the temptation of "playing it safe" to insulate himself. "I once read that some men will avoid meeting one to one with women in their office or over a meal," Robert mused. "It'll be hard to coach Yvonne if I only do it with an audience!" Robert realized, just as Maria did when she approached Alvin, that exploring the elephant requires courage and "playing it safe" doesn't grow earned advantage. The courage Robert, and those with more unearned advantage, need to recognize and work with the elephant requires compassion – for self and for others. He, and all the team, need the courage to grow through trial and error as they learn. This is also part of the elephant.

Calling up and sustaining the courage to explore the elephant isn't easy. As we've seen, all our characters, and each of us, will at different points unintentionally react with an emotional response of fight, flee, appease, or freeze. As we've seen, these reactions are natural to all of us. And to be clear, when it comes to seeing or experiencing injustice or unfairness, emotional responses, particularly fight, are natural and can be fuel for intentional action. Mindful courage in the face of injustice, whether unintentional micro-aggression in the office or historic, systemic discrimination in a society, requires standing up to injustice with intentional action. How does a person grow courage? How does one choose when, where, and how to stand up?

In this book, we have focused on a team of people in everyday situations facing various intersections of unearned advantage, others and their own. Depending on who you are and where you're from, you may, like Robert, want to build courage to face your own unearned advantages – that is a powerful start. Perhaps, you might also support others like yourself who are facing these challenges. Finally, you might engage and support those with fewer opportunities for earned advantage. If you have a few or many fewer unearned advantages, like Alvin, Maria, or Yvonne, you may want to build courage to engage those with more unearned advantages while supporting those with fewer to grow opportunities for earned advantage.

Finding and developing *courage* to explore the elephant isn't easy – but it is possible with practice. It comes more naturally to some than others for reasons of personality as well as lived experiences. Like intention setting, practicing courage when it's not needed develops the mental and emotional muscles needed when it is needed. Scholars and experts have written countless articles and books on how to develop courage (see some in the Additional Reading section). Here are some steps you can practice:

1. Recognize it – the half-empty glass. When exploring the elephant, realize that we all at first see what can hurt us. We defend against it, whether it's likely or not. "Hope for the best, prepare for the worst" is, as the team says, not a strategy. This old saying hurts rather than helps by inflating negatives and directing attention away from positives.

2. Imagine it. Like Alvin did. Play out a scenario in your mind where you engage someone with different advantages. Explore the best, worst, and most-likely outcomes and what intentions you can set for the best.

3. Talk about it. So often, sharing our doubts and fears makes them easier to address. Talking it over also gives perspective and the opportunity to learn from

others who have faced similar challenges. As you have probably found in your own experience, when you say things out loud, they are easier to understand.

4. Work with it. Courage accepts both the fear in exploring the elephant of unearned advantage and the greater value of growing earned advantage for everyone. With practice sustained by courage, you are able to spend less time in the comfort zone, more time in the growth zone, and manage the inevitable trips into the overwhelm zone.

5. Grow it. Whatever your role is, no matter who you are or where you're from, no matter how fixed or growth your mindset may be, there's opportunity to grow. Whether you have many or few tailwinds or headwinds, there's opportunity to grow. Courage begins and sustains exploring the elephant and it grows with use.

Without doubt, as you read this book, you found some ideas and suggestions uncomfortable or awkward. As you reflect on that, you may recognize that this reaction is a natural, even unavoidable, part of growing. Exploring the elephant and growing earned advantage stretches each of us. How productive would it be if everyone could see color-ful without trying to be color blind? What if gender and identity were valued for unique contributions and still with inclusion? What would it mean for performance if all the differences in who you are and where you're from were recognized and worked with? Since we each still see only part of the elephant, we have to explore.

As we said before, this won't be without missteps and mistakes – explorers get it right the first time by luck. Explorers, leaving aside those exploring to take what's not theirs, have the courage to make attempts as much as the courage to learn to "get it right." Regardless of your levels of unearned advantage, building courage is essential. There are, however, some final, useful reflections to consider depending on your levels of unearned advantage. With a spirit of recognizing, working with, and growing, we recommend you reflect on what's next for those with more and those with less unearned advantage.

What's next? If you hold more unearned advantage

As you explore the elephant, you may be afraid of running into pointed tusks, snapping tails, stomping feet, and loud trumpets as you make missteps or mistakes. Like anything else that's scary or difficult, we imagine worst-case scenarios that prevent us from taking the first step. Developing resilience and compassion will help you avoid fighting, fleeing, freezing, or appeasing as that happens. Growing earned advantage in the ways described in this book is an outcome of individual effort that only happens with that effort. Whatever unearned advantage you have, even if only a little, recognizing and working with it will be challenging. Those with little may find it challenging to see even that little amount because it is little compared to others. However, it is there and worthy of exploring. Those with more unearned advantage have a different, but equally difficult, challenge – the fear of losing it.

A fear common to those with unearned advantages is, "What will I lose, if I open myself to reflecting on these questions?" Robert realized he couldn't give back his unearned advantage and set out to grow earned advantage in the ways he could. He applied the Growth Advantage Mindset. But the Fixed Advantage Mindset often believes there is a limited supply of opportunity for earned advantage and that "they" want to take away that opportunity to balance it out.

It's easy to be afraid of "them" – whoever they are. Politics, culture, and policy of every age are shaped by "me," "us," "them," and "others." The apparent increasing divisions of the 21st century that motivated this book are based on who you are and where you're from. The tension between belonging and uniqueness isn't new and can foster innovation and creativity if it can be managed by each of us. Respecting and being respected for uniqueness is part of belonging and doesn't require sacrificing anything more than the comfort of the Fixed Advantage Mindset.

The Fixed Advantage Mindset also suggests that an individual can't possibly make enough difference to change an entire society, especially when the rules, written or not, work to one degree or another in our favor. Growing the elephant happens one person at a time – with you. You aren't being tasked to change the world of unearned advantage but to increase the opportunity for earned advantage – one interaction at a time. The Growth Advantage Mindset sees the potential for improvement on a scale it can manage.

What's next? If you hold or support less unearned advantage

If you hold less unearned advantage, you may or may not have been surprised that those with more unearned advantage have to work through that reality. As you work with and grow earned advantage and engage those with more unearned advantage, you may also find yourself to be feared or, possibly, experienced as the tusk, tail, legs, or trunk as others make their missteps and mistakes. Whether you hold less unearned advantage or are an advocate or ally for those who hold less, tolerance for your own inexpert efforts and those of others also requires resilience and compassion. Calling people in for dialogue to increase awareness and understanding – to explore the elephant – is as necessary as calling people out for acting with unearned advantage. Those with less unearned advantage and their advocates also face a specific fight/flee/freeze/appease challenge – the challenge to productively engage.

Like those with many unearned advantages, those with few also ask, "What will I lose, if I open myself to engaging?" Through the book, team members with less unearned advantage developed approaches to gain earned advantage. Alvin shared, Maria engaged, Yvonne asked. Maria had a moment where she wondered why she needed to explain why Carl asking about lunch wasn't appropriate and Yvonne was reminded that her strong communication skills surprised Alex. If either Maria or Yvonne held their silence, neither Carl nor Alex would have taken note.

These seem like tiny gains in a world of powerful headwinds and tailwinds. While those with unearned advantage may fear losing something, those without it already have the lived experiences of being with less. The Growth Advantage Mindset, however, posits that there is an unlimited supply of opportunity for earned advantage and, through persistent engagement, it can be balanced. No doubt, significant change is needed to balance it for everyone and the saying, "Better to light one candle than curse the darkness" sounds hollow when headwinds keep blowing it out. Courage is key – because it's easy to be afraid.

It's easy and not illogical for those with less unearned advantage to be afraid of "them" – individuals, groups, and systems supporting unearned advantage. History provides too many examples to pretend otherwise. Those holding or supporting less unearned advantage are justified in being skeptical of efforts or the potential to grow earned advantage. Managing expectations is perfectly natural and reasonable. You can, however, set intentions to grow from a Fixed Advantage Mindset to a Growth Advantage Mindset and grow the elephant – including for yourself.

The Fixed Advantage Mindset suggests that an individual can't possibly make enough difference to change an entire society, or even one's own experience. By now, we hope you see that growing the elephant happens one person at a time – with you. You aren't being tasked to change the world of unearned advantage but to increase the opportunity, your own and others, for earned advantage one opportunity at a time. Again, the Growth Advantage Mindset sees the potential for improvement on a scale it can manage.

Final thoughts

Whoever you are and wherever you're from, you've been exploring the elephant in the room – the elephant of advantage. However many or few unearned advantages you have, you've been recognizing and working with unearned advantage and, we hope, seen the potential and even begun growing opportunities for earned advantage – for everyone. Most people don't start this journey and not all who start explore this far – congratulations!

As we said at the start, this is uncomfortable and requires courage – the willingness to face what's difficult and even scary. It requires a growth mindset – the willingness to attempt, fail, and learn. It also requires intention – your stated what and your stated why – to explore it with purpose. And it requires awareness – self, other, and self-on-other – to manage the inevitable challenges that come with facing trumpeting trunks, stomping legs, slicing ears, and whipping tails. It requires a lot – and so, it begs the question, "Is it worth it?"

When we set out to write this book, it was an attempt to rethink and reframe how we talk and think about issues of diversity, equity, and inclusion and, specifically, privilege. We sought to include a variety of contemplative reflections that help readers leverage their own lived experiences to understand and relate to those of other people. From that understanding and with some practical examples, we sought to give each reader different ways to share and grow opportunities for earned advantage from whatever unearned advantages they may have.

In writing this book, we imagined some people exploring it on their own and some people exploring with others. For those exploring it on their own, we imagined them actually doing the exercises rather than reading about them. We imagined them sharing what they learn in ways that work for them. We imagined individuals willing to challenge themselves and grow from it. We imagined small, tentative steps that, with practice, grow into longer, confident strides. We imagined people reading this book in more than one sitting to allow for reflection, and revisiting their notes both for themselves and for others.

For those exploring it with others, we imagined people with a lot in common working together as well as people with less in common, sharing their experiences and perceptions and practicing non-judgmental ways. Unlike the unproductive DEI training experience described at the beginning of this book, as well as the countless examples in the media of people channeling their energy into shouting, fighting, or worse, we imagined productive discussions where people meet and are met wherever they are with an openness that comes with practice. We imagined an incremental, but steady, increase of understanding and compassion. We imagined increases in collaboration, innovation, and productivity in groups truly leveraging the power of diversity and inclusion.

In case these ruminations feel more dreamy than realistic, please reconsider. We offer these scenarios because we have lived them and have seen progress. As board members, executives, or consultants to both, we have experienced these scenarios where "improving DEI" was the goal. But we have also experienced them when effective DEI was understood as a path to a goal, like effective business performance, board governance, or executive development. Other goals supported through effective DEI include strengthened organizational culture, refined measures of strategy and performance, or bolstered community impact and resource development. In our respective roles in higher education, the scenarios often involved students and leaders wrestling to connect theory to practice and managing differing and even conflicting points of view. Like everyone else concerned about growing earned advantage, they wrestled to establish that ever elusive set of metrics or indicators of diversity, equity, and inclusion that mattered most. For all the focus on metrics and programs, however, what has been too often underestimated and insufficiently developed is the power of the individual. That's why we focus in this book on individual readers.

On you.

Whether working with board members, executives, staff, volunteers, or community leaders, it is clear from our shared experiences that these individuals during important stages of their lives had taken time to re-think and re-frame. For some, we observe that theirs had been a lifelong practice. For others – maybe most – we see that some event or life experience prompted awareness and intention to move; deciding to be and do differently to create more opportunities for all. In every case, one key individual joins forces with others and change begins.

Imagine if each person you knew were to grow even the smallest example of earned advantage. Imagine how quickly opportunities for earned advantage would multiply if unearned advantages were broadly shared. Imagine what each person could contribute and achieve by growing earned advantage – whoever you are and wherever you're from.

And now consider, is it worth it?

Epilogue

At the crumbled close of the failed DEI session in the Prologue each of our team felt as do many participants in these programs: one or more of spotlighted, lectured to, generalized, ignored, or called out. Even the trainer lamented not having a GPS for a path leading to a better destination of collaboration, innovation, belonging, and uniqueness. "Even though we all work together, it seems like we're all in a different place," she said. And, of course, she was right about that.

When observed in their natural environments, people are amazed at how quietly and quickly elephants can move across the landscape. And, while they can trumpet and stomp loudly, they also communicate with sounds we can't hear and through nuanced movements we can't see. On top of that, elephants, like us, each have their own personality and lived experiences. Elephants are known to travel hundreds and even thousands of miles over the same routes (without GPS). It's all very natural to elephants – including the elephant of advantage. All we humans have to do is to get past what we think we know about the elephant to see it as it actually is.

In this story, each member of our team, along with some others, began to explore the elephant and grow opportunities for earned advantage. They learned to notice that people often maintain the status quo – the persistence of unearned advantage – simply because the landscape and routes seem familiar, because navigating those familiar spaces requires less time and effort. They learned that intentionally increasing earned advantage for more people actually can feel unnatural, yet they persisted. They didn't change the entire world all at once or ever. They didn't find everything easy ever after and they still witnessed or experienced examples of unfairness and injustice – some annoying and some horrific. They did, however, each in their own way, find moments and situations to recognize and work with unearned advantage to grow opportunities for earned advantage. Sometimes they made mistakes and sometimes they found it hard to get past the mistakes of others. But with practice, they each found they had an impact on and beyond themselves. With practice, each found they could grow earned advantage – one person at a time – for others in their life.

Resources

Exploring the elephant isn't easy! We have developed some additional resources to support you on your journey. We provide some in this book and an increasing number on the book's website www.growingtheelephant.com.

Audio recordings

Guided audio recordings of the reflections and exercises in this book and some others are provided free on the book's website. Check them out!

How to eat an elephant? A plan for one bite at a time...

A famous quote associated with many smart people, including Archbishop Desmond Tutu, is that you tackle a difficult challenge like you'd eat an elephant: one bite at a time. There are many ways to approach consulting *Growing the Elephant* – here are some ideas:

- Set and meet an intention to read through and practice at least one reflection exercise at least once a week. If you're a fast reader, ride the elephant as quickly as you prefer, and then return to the weekly cadence.

- Make a journal to capture your thoughts, feelings, insights, concerns – anything that feels relevant to you. If you set an intention to do more, less, or to continue any particular behavior of words or actions (from self-on-other awareness), write it down.
- Our pre-publication readers often found that their most useful insights followed their initial emotional reactions. When you find something difficult to accept (or allow), see if you can suspend judgment or conclusion and let it sit a while.
- Some people find it easier to talk over what they are finding with trusted others – sometimes others like themselves, sometimes others different from themselves. Set an intention to share what you're learning and learn from someone else once a week.
- Some people find they want to talk over what they are finding with a group – sometimes a group like them (homogenous), sometimes a mixed group (heterogenous). Visit the *Growing the Elephant* website to develop an approach to discussing with groups.

Dynamics of advantage

Advantage, earned and unearned, has many attributes. Our ability to recognize and work with unearned advantage enables our ability to grow opportunities for earned advantage for all. This summary of dynamics of advantage can be a touchstone to remind you of how advantage works:

- Those with less unearned advantage may gain earned advantage – but it takes more work, talent, support, etc., compared to those holding more unearned advantage.

- Those with less unearned advantage are at greater risk of losing what earned advantage they have gained.
- Those with more unearned advantage cannot lose it, "give it back," or have it taken away, but they can lend it or apply it on behalf of those without it.
- Those with less unearned advantage cannot take it from those with more.
- The opportunity to earn advantage is not equitably distributed because unearned advantage takes a share.
- Unearned advantage can accrue to the majority in representation or the minority–majority in wealth, power, or influence.
- The deliberate manipulation of advantage in any community or society occurs. However, the status quo of advantage is more reinforced by unconscious biases and cultural practices and traditions. Awareness matters and individuals can make a difference.

Unconscious biases – the Implicit Association Test

As Robert and many others found, taking the IAT is a challenging exercise of awareness. You can try it out here. While it's free to take, it may cost you some complacency or comfort. https://implicit.harvard.edu/implicit/takeatest.html

Dimensions of power

Dimensions of Power is a framework for understanding how transformation to achieve more diversity/equity/inclusion in complex organizations requires increasing degrees of power sharing. Listed to show the highest impact of DEI intentionality, the dimensions are 1) Setting organizational priorities regarding messaging, people, and money; 2) Seeking diverse perspectives including perspectives of underrepresented population groups (those without unearned advantage) before final decisions are made; and 3) Aiming for diverse representation physically of underrepresented population groups. Researchers have found that most organizations increase their effectiveness when their leadership teams are powered by a diversity of perspectives that often emanates from diversity in terms of race, ethnicity, age, ability, and gender. This is true in business, the charitable sector, the public sector, and higher education. For more information, contact Gloria Johnson-Cusack at Gloria Johnson-Cusack Consulting, LLC.

Additional reading

Along with the sources noted in footnotes, we've compiled some of the reading that informed our book and that we've found helpful.

Books

Chugh, Dolly (2018). *The Person You Mean to Be: How Good People Fight Bias.* HarperCollins.

Dweck, Carol (2006). *Mindset: The New Psychology of Success.* Random House.

Hanson, Rick (2018). *Resilient: Find Your Inner Strength.* Penguin/Random House.

Johnson, Stefanie K. (2020). *Inclusify: The Power of Uniqueness and Belonging to Build Innovative Teams.* Harper Business.

Kabat-Zinn, Jon (2013). *Full Catastrophe Living: Using the Wisdom of Your Body and Mind to Face Stress, Pain, and Illness.* Bantam.

Magee, Rhonda (2019). *The Inner Work of Racial Justice: Healing Ourselves and Transforming Our Communities Through Mindfulness.* TarcherPerigree.

National Committee for Responsive Philanthropy, authored by Lisa Ranghelli and Jennifer Choi with Dan Petegorsky, Caitlin Duffy, and Stephanie Peng (2018). *Power Moves: Your Essential Philanthropy Assessment Guide for Equity and Justice.*

Treleaven, David (2018). *Trauma-Sensitive Mindfulness: Practices for Safe and Transformative Healing.* W. W. Norton.

Winston, Diana (2019). *The Little Book of Being: Practices and Guidance for Uncovering Your Natural Awareness.* Sounds True.

Articles

Dweck, Carol (2016). "What having a 'growth mindset' actually means," *Harvard Business Review,* January 13, 2016. Available from https://hbr.org/2016/01/what-having-a-growth-mindset-actually-means [accessed May 5, 2022].

Gassam Asare, Janice. (2021). "How the adultification bias contributes to Black trauma," *Forbes,* April 22, 2021. Available from www.forbes.com/sites/janicegassam/2021/04/22/how-the-adultification-bias-contributes-to-black-trauma/ [accessed May 5, 2022].

Gonzalez-Barrera, Ana (2019). "Hispanics with darker skin are more likely to experience racial discrimination than those with lighter skin." Pew Research Center. Available from www.pewresearch.org/fact-tank/2019/07/02/hispanics-with-darker-skin-are-more-likely-to-experience-discrimination-than-those-with-lighter-skin/ [accessed May 5, 2022].

Kets de Vries, Manfred F. R. (2020). "How to find and practice courage," *Harvard Business Review,* May 12, 2020. Available from https://hbr.org/2020/05/how-to-find-and-practice-courage [accessed May 5, 2022].

Magee, Rhonda (2015). "How mindfulness can defeat racial bias." *Greater Good Magazine,* May 14, 2015. Available from https://greatergood.berkeley.edu/article/item/how_mindfulness_can_defeat_racial_bias [accessed May 5, 2022].

National Association of School Psychologists (2016). "Understanding Race and Privilege" [handout].

Glossary

*W*e've listed here some of the most important concepts and practices suggested in this book. You might find it helpful to refer to this glossary regularly as you read, reflect, and discuss with others.

Concepts

Advantage – a superiority of position or condition; a factor or circumstance of benefit to its possessor.[1]

- **Earned advantage** – benefits or position gained or granted based on what you do without regard to who you are.
- **Unearned advantage** – benefits or position gained or granted by virtue of who you are or where you're from. Also known as "Privilege."

Advantage Mindset – a set of beliefs about and typical reactions to concepts of advantage defined as "fixed" – not inclined to attempt something new and risk failure, thereby reducing learning opportunity, versus "growth" – inclined to attempt something new and risk failure, thereby increasing

---

[1] Merriam-Webster, Definition of "advantage", 2021. Available from www.merriam-webster.com/dictionary/advantage [accessed May 5, 2022].

learning (growth) opportunity; adapted and based on the work of Carol Dweck.

Diversity – the range of human differences across traits of who you are, including gender, race, age, ability, sexual identity, appearance, and personality, and where you're from, including where and how you grew up or moved from, and the total range of your lived experiences.

Equity – the consistent and systematic fair, just, and impartial treatment of all individuals by other individuals and the community, "achieved when you can no longer predict an advantage or disadvantage based on who you are or where you're from."[2]

Inclusion – meeting the fundamental, and occasionally conflicting, human needs of belongingness and uniqueness; respecting being part of a community and being an individual, and providing space and opportunity to meet both of those needs, achieved when "individuals are able to participate fully in the decision-making processes within an organization or group."[3]

Privilege – also known as unearned advantage, a right or immunity granted as a peculiar benefit, advantage, or favor by virtue of who you are or where you're from; an unearned advantage that cannot be returned, taken away, replaced, or refunded. It can be lent or its benefits shared.

---

[2] National Committee for Responsive Philanthropy, *Power Moves: Your Essential Philanthropy Assessment Guide for Equity and Justice*, p. 65.
[3] Ibid.

Winds ahead and behind

Headwind – a wind having the opposite general direction to a course of movement (as of an aircraft); a force or influence that slows progress to an improved condition.[4] In terms of unearned advantage, any attribute of who you are or where you're from that, more often than not, requires more effort or support to achieve success compared to someone without that attribute.

Tailwind – a wind having the same general direction as a course of movement (as of an aircraft); a force or influence that advances progress toward an improved condition.[5] In terms of unearned advantage, any attribute of who you are or where you're from that, more often than not, provides support or reduces required effort to achieve success compared to someone without that attribute.

Practices

Calling out, calling in

Calling out – to "issue a direct challenge to something they've said or done, usually in public and with the intent of exposing the person's wrongdoing to others."

---

[4] Merriam-Webster, Definition of "headwind," 2022. Available from www.merriam-webster.com/dictionary/headwind [accessed April 13, 2022].
[5] Merriam-Webster, Definition of "tailwind," 2022. Available from www.merriam-webster.com/dictionary/tailwind [accessed April 13, 2022].

Calling in – refers to "the act of checking your peers and getting them to change problematic behavior by explaining their misstep with compassion and patience."[6]

Compassion – a practice of combining your genuine empathy for someone's (or your own) plight with a (set and met) intention to act to improve the situation. Cited experts include Sharon Salzberg and Kristin Neff.

Intention – a practice of stating, even to yourself, the combination of your desired outcome – your what, with the reason you want that outcome – your why. Intentions increase accountability and the potential for success, especially when shared.

Mindfulness – the ability to be fully present and self-aware in the current moment without being overwhelmed by negative emotions. Experts cited in this book include Jon Kabat-Zinn and author Diana Winston of UCLA's Mindful Awareness Research Center. UCLA offers its own mindfulness curricula, including Mindful Awareness Practices (MAPS).

Mindfulness-Based Stress Reduction – Maria refers to MBSR, an eight-week non-religious, mindfulness training program created by Jon Kabat-Zinn in 1979 at the University of Massachusetts Medical Center. Focusing on meditation and mindful movement and initially created for chronically ill patients who were not responding well to traditional

---

[6] Ashley Austrew, "Is there a difference between 'calling in' and 'calling out'?" *Dictionary.com*, March 22, 2019. Available from www.dictionary.com/e/calling-in-vs-calling-out/ [accessed May 5, 2022].

treatments, it is now used for a wide variety of reasons to increase people's ability to manage their response to stress.

RAIN – a compassion practice of Recognize, Accept, Investigate with Natural Awareness (or Nurture) to be present with uncomfortable situations, like recognizing and working with unearned advantage; created by Michele McDonald and expanded by Tara Brach, Diana Winston, and others.

STOP – a stress-management practice of Stop, Take a breath, Observe what's actually happening, and then Proceed taught in various stress-management programs, including MBSR and UCLA's Mindful Awareness Practices (MAPS) curricula.

About the authors

Chris Altizer, MA, MBA

A retired, recovering HR executive with every unearned advantage short of height, Chris now consults and coaches executives globally and teaches at Florida International University College of Business and the FIU Center for Leadership. He has led leadership teams and worked with CEOs and senior leaders around the globe across diverse industries, including healthcare, insurance, and consumer products.

From this privileged position, he joins Gloria in addressing the elephant in the room – the elephant of unearned advantage.

Chris's unusual combination of experiences as a business leader and mindfulness teacher have greatly influenced his work in diversity, equity, and inclusion. Dissatisfied with current approaches and facing a polarized landscape, he invites readers to experiment with well-researched, non-religious contemplative practices to help them explore the elephant of unearned advantage and grow the elephant of earned advantage – for all.

A published author, researcher, and cited expert in human resources, Chris holds an MBA with honors from Columbia University, MAHRD from Northeastern Illinois University, and BA from Hampden-Sydney College, as well as MBSR teacher qualification through UC San Diego. He is a certified yoga teacher and 5th degree black belt martial artist, disciplines he has enjoyed learning, practicing, and teaching alongside his wife and two sons.

Gloria Johnson-Cusack, MPA

A changemaker who has been an executive in philanthropy, government, academia, business, and nonprofit sectors, Gloria Johnson-Cusack was the former Senior Advisor to the President of Florida International University, is Board Chair of the Firelight Foundation supporting communities in Africa, and consultant to leadership teams and boards. She is a speaker, lecturer, and servant leader providing strategic counsel to leadership teams and boards globally regarding diversity/equity/inclusion, governance, change leadership, and strategic planning for resource development and advocacy.

As a person of African-American and Haliwa-Saponi ancestry, Gloria came from a segregated background in the United States and moved from being middle class to working-poor to decidedly privileged. From and through this journey, Gloria aims to use her lived experience to build bridges.

Gloria has a wide range of professional experiences across academia, government, and non-profit sectors. She served as a lobbyist for the charitable sector, Executive Director of Leadership 18 (an alliance of 18+ CEOs responsible for leading national nonprofit organizations), Board Chair of National United Cerebral Palsy, Director of the Office of Congressional Relations at the U.S. Peace Corps, Senior VP for a cause-marketing advertising firm, and Special Assistant to the President in the White House Office of National Service. She has served as adjunct lecturer at Columbia University in New York. Gloria holds graduate and undergraduate degrees from American University and Columbia University.

Acknowledgements

Chris

If anyone would've said, even just a few years ago, that I'd be writing a book like this, I wouldn't have believed it (nor would many others). But the seeds have been there, planted, or cultivated by my wife Anne, sons Connor and Ryan, and my siblings and parents. I also thank my teachers of karate, yoga, and mindfulness and the many friends and colleagues who influenced or informed me even when I didn't realize it (or thanked them). Like Robert, I'm still learning. With gratitude, I thank the many who challenged what I thought I knew and provided background and insight for this project. I must also thank those who still teach me today, including the experts cited in the book, and especially Rhonda V. Magee, Dave Ulrich, and my co-author Gloria.

Gloria

The most important person to thank is my co-author, Chris, who conceived this book, did the heaviest lifting and writing, and was a super gracious collaborator. For the Christian values that compel me to love ALL and to the close family and friends who live out this love so powerfully in my life, I am thankful. Thanks to Chief Richardson, of the Haliwa Saponi Indian tribe, the first woman to hold that title for our tribe and a continuous source of inspiration. To my bossy buddy, Jill Black Zalben, I am keeping my promise to name you because you urged me to "start one of your books" and introduced me to the meditation practice that complements my prayer life to this day. And, to all the clients and fellow do-gooders – past, present, and future – thank you for helping us ground this work in current realities even as we imagine BETTER.

Index

CPSIA information can be obtained
at www.ICGtesting.com
Printed in the USA
JSHW032249281022
32324JS00002B/4